Food Refusal and Avoidant Eating in Children, including those with Autism Spectrum Conditions

A Practical Guide for Parents and Professionals

Gillian Harris and Elizabeth Shea

Jessica Kingsley *Publishers*
London and Philadelphia

First published in 2018
by Jessica Kingsley Publishers
73 Collier Street
London N1 9BE, UK
and
400 Market Street, Suite 400
Philadelphia, PA 19106, USA

www.jkp.com

Library of Congress Cataloging in Publication Data
A CIP catalog record for this book is available from the Library of Congress

British Library Cataloguing in Publication Data
A CIP catalogue record for this book is available from the British Library

ISBN 978 1 78592 318 0
eISBN 978 1 78450 632 2

Printed and bound in Great Britain

To my children, Holly, Fern and Maddy, who have put up with my shortcomings as a parent, to Bertie who doesn't think that I have any shortcomings and to Peter who married me despite my shortcomings.

For my parents who helped me get that first job and for Phillip who means I never have to cook again.

Acknowledgments

We would like to acknowledge the expertise of our colleague Sarah Mason who worked as a lead Speech and Language Therapist in dysphagia at the Children's Hospital, Birmingham. Her knowledge, input and collaboration have been invaluable. She has taught us all that we know about the physical act of eating and swallowing, and she has also often shown us how to work with sensory-sensitive children. Many of her tips on desensitisation are included in the book.

We would also like to mention our research colleagues, Jackie Blissett, Helen Coulthard, Claire Farrow, Emma Haycraft and Jason Thomas. Their research and insightful comments underpin all that we do.

In addition we wish to acknowledge colleagues at the National Autistic Society and its branch associations and Charlene Tait of Scottish Autism for their support of our work on eating in autistic young people.

Lastly, we wish to thank all of those children and their families with whom we have worked. They have taught us most of what we know about avoidant eating.

Notes on the text

Throughout the book we use the terms 'autistic child/teenager' and 'on the autism spectrum' for consistency when referring to this group of young people. This reflects recent research on the preferences of autistic people for the language used to describe them.

Contents

Introduction 9

**Part 1. Acceptance and Rejection of New Foods
in Infancy and Childhood: Development Stages** 15

1. The Early Stages 17
2. Neophobia: The Onset of the Fear of New and
   Different Foods 34
3. Sensory Factors and How These Affect Food
   Acceptance 51
4. The Disgust Response and the Development of
   Avoidant Eating 64
5. Appetite and Appetite Regulation 79
6. What Is Avoidant and Restrictive Food Intake
   Disorder? 95

**Part 2. Avoidant and Restrictive Eating:
Strategies and Interventions** 111

7. Managing the Environment around the Child 113
8. Is the Child Ready to Move On? 126
9. What Doesn't Work and Why 139
10. Interventions with the Younger Child 153
11. Interventions with the Older Child 175
12. What Else Might Be Going Wrong? 195

Final Words 211
Bibliography 212
Resources 221
Index 223

Introduction

Dr Gillian Harris

I am very lucky to have two children who ate very well; they were not particularly fussy and would eat most things given to them. One of the two was more experimental perhaps and enjoyed her food more than the other, but neither of them posed a problem for me. They grew well; they would eat home-prepared food and were happy with school dinners. They both slept well; their behaviour was just as you would expect from two typical infants and toddlers.

What did I do to deserve these two easy eaters? Nothing; I was just lucky. Not so, though, with my first child. I was very young when they sent me home with my first baby. I couldn't really believe that they would just pack me off with this unknown entity, and without the user's manual, and leave me alone at home to look after her. But they did, and so I learned my trade the hard way, by experience. My first daughter didn't want to eat; she didn't want milk, and when the time came to introduce solid foods, she didn't want those either. She would eat one kind of baby fruit puree and possibly some boiled egg. If I left a few raisins on her tray and didn't look at her, she would occasionally eat those. I took her to the health visitors; she was growing fine, no problem. What I didn't realise was that she was small for a term baby, always bumping along the bottom centile lines of the growth charts and never destined to be tall. She doesn't quite make five foot now as an adult, so she didn't need as much food as it said in the books and leaflets that I pored over. And she was sensory-hypersensitive, so destined to be extremely fussy as well. I dreaded mealtimes; I would insist that my husband got home in time for her tea. It took two of us to coax her to eat even a little, but at least it was less stressful with someone else there. There were other things that were different as well. She hated being cuddled or held. She could not be soothed to sleep, and she would cry for hours when tired. The only thing that worked was driving her round in the car until she finally gave in, or racing along the pavement with her in her pram. Her baby photos show a happy, chubby, healthy baby. Her mummy photos show someone very anxious, and very worn out.

As she grew older, she continued to be 'fussy'. She would eat nothing mixed and nothing slimy. Fish and mushrooms were definitely out. If I chopped them very small, she still found them. One evening her father tried to be strict and insist she ate some fish. She refused, she was sent to her room and she stayed there. She would rather go without than eat it, so we never tried that again. She went to school with her carefully packed lunches, disliked the smell of other people's food and was wary of new foods. She was an anxious child, easily upset by changes in routine and environment. Luckily, she went to a small local school, she learned to read at an early age and gradually all changed for the better.

This was well over 40 years ago, and as my career in psychology gradually progressed, my interest moved from developmental psychology to eating behaviour in children. Why didn't they eat? Why was it always the mother's fault (in those days it was always the mother)? My other children ate well, so what was it about my firstborn? And why did she line up cars that she had collected and ask for a garage rather than dolls? She was impossible to get to sleep at nights. Her father and I would fall asleep reading to her. She would stay awake, playing quietly over our sleeping bodies. Eventually, at midnight she might drop off, but at 4am she would be up again in our bed, running her cars and trucks up and down my sleeping body. She was such an escape artist that we put her into a bed rather than a cot at an early age. So what was going on? She couldn't be on the spectrum, because 'girls didn't have Asperger's syndrome'. And why is it that now she is an excellent and experimental cook, trying new things? My other children remember with horror the rather limited diet that they all had to eat as she got older, many meals involving frozen crispy cheese pancakes, a well-known convenience food at the time. So yes, for some time it did affect family life, but I was lucky. The eating problems resolved, and by late childhood she was eating a reasonably wide and acceptable range of foods. She could take a packed lunch to school and eat with us when we went out for meals.

I had by then started research into infant and children's food acceptance and refusal, when I was asked to help a colleague (a gastroenterologist), because he had children attending his clinics who were vomiting at mealtimes, or refusing to eat, with no medical or physical cause. My involvement in these clinics led to my decision to train as clinician. For the rest of my working life I was lucky enough to work as a clinician with infants and children who couldn't or wouldn't eat, while also carrying out research to underpin my clinical work and interventions. I was also fortunate to be able to work in joint clinics with Sarah Mason, and this too increased my knowledge base. I have learned much from my research and clinical colleagues, but mostly I have learned what I know from the children I have met along the way. I also know what it feels like to be a parent faced with a child who just won't eat, and the children in my clinic have made me aware of what it is like to be faced with food that you just can't eat, surrounded by adults who are desperate that you should eat it. Adults so desperate that they will force you, coax you, plead with you – anything to get that food down. So although I sympathise with the parents of the children I have worked with, my starting point in any intervention has always been from where the child is, starting with what they could eat, what they could cope with, and moving on with them from there.

Dr Elizabeth Shea

I like to solve puzzles and one of the most enduring and interesting for me during my career has been working out why people on the autism spectrum eat the way they do and what we can do about it.

This interest began at the start of my psychology career. I came to psychology via a varied path that had taken me to art school, primary school teaching, working in museums, libraries, in business and in counselling children. When I finally settled on psychology, I landed my first 'real' job with the National

Autistic Society working as a care worker in a residential school. Back then, I knew very little about autism and even less about the psychology of eating. Nevertheless, my first task on my first day in the new job was to cook dinner for eight young men on the spectrum.

I wasn't much of a cook back then (and I'm still not!), but – fortunately – scheduled on the menu that night was what I then considered to be my signature dish of spaghetti bolognaise. What could possibly go wrong? Having negotiated the unfamiliarity of a large industrial kitchen, I soon proudly presented my masterpiece to the young men in my care and was surprised and flummoxed as to what happened next. Some of them ate it; in fact, one of them ate it so quickly that I was worried he would choke. Some of them initially refused it but could be coaxed into eating once I'd pointed out there were no hidden vegetables! But one young man was having none of it and flatly refused. Like me, he was new to the school, and because he was non-verbal, I struggled to work out what was wrong with my delicious dish. After ten minutes of plate tennis (I pushed the plate towards him, he pushed it back), I went back to the kitchen to see what else I could find. Searching in the cupboards, I was rewarded with a tin of Heinz spaghetti hoops (other brands are available but, as you will see later, won't always do) and a loaf of bread. I made spaghetti hoops on toast and to my immense relief he ate the lot. Phew!

Day two in the new job, and I was back on cooking duties – this time a cottage pie. More or less the same things happened. Some of the young people ate it, some were initially reluctant, and one young man ate it and then regurgitated it, spitting it up high on to the ceiling. My particular young man again flatly refused to try it. Not bothering to play plate tennis again, I dug out another tin of spaghetti hoops (same brand), and he ate the same meal as the night before. Now, this went on for a couple of weeks, with him every night refusing to eat anything other than the aforementioned brand of spaghetti hoops on toast. One day we didn't have Heinz, so I substituted a different brand; he refused this on sight. How could he possibly tell? On a couple of occasions, I overcooked the toast, which he then also refused. I soon learnt it had to be the right brand of hoops, and the toast had to be cooked and presented in exactly the same way before he would eat it. Eventually, getting more and more puzzled about why he was refusing everything else, I spoke to his teacher and to his parents. What I learnt was that he ate a few, very specific foods at school, at home and when he went to respite, and that these foods never crossed context. He never, for example, ate the same foods at home that he ate in respite and, what's more, spaghetti hoops were a brand-new food for him.

It was only some years later, and after learning much more about how we develop our eating skills and food preferences, that I understood the significance of what had happened with him. We are all likely to eat something new when in a new environment, and young people on the spectrum in particular appear to store the food and the context as one whole experience. If we add to that difficulties generalising from one situation to another and sensory sensitivities, meaning that mixed textures (think spaghetti bolognaise) are often rejected, we can start to understand why he ate the same foods every day. He rejected my spaghetti, then simply ate what I gave him that first night instead (which was also a meal of 'beige carbohydrates', but more of that later) and then ate it every night afterwards. Over the course of the next year I did manage to get him to eat some different things, but these were always brand-new foods, and they were only ever accepted when we were doing a new activity. He never ate my spaghetti bolognaise, my cottage pie or any other brand of spaghetti hoops.

My career then took a dual direction, with me working across the fields of autism and childhood feeding disorders and developing a career-long interest in restricted and avoidant eating, particularly in individuals on the autism spectrum. However, I've always remembered the experience I gained in that first job, and, I hope, this has helped me in my daily work with families.

So for the parents who are reading this book, I want you to know I've been where you've been. I've cooked for avoidant teenagers, and I know what it's like when the lovingly prepared and healthy meal is refused. It triggers anxiety and panic – 'But what can I give them instead?' and 'What if they don't eat anything?' – and feelings of despair – 'They'll get seriously ill and it'll be my fault.' I learnt that it was not my fault but a part of their autism. I hope reading this book will help you learn that too.

Part 1

Acceptance and Rejection of New Foods in Infancy and Childhood
Development Stages

Introduction to Part 1

The first part of the book introduces the developmental stages behind the acceptance and rejection of new foods in infancy and childhood. All of the information outlined in this part of the book is 'evidence-based'; it describes research studies that have been carried out on children's or adult's eating behaviour.

We describe normal development in feeding, but also talk about those children who are often termed 'fussy'. To begin with, we do use this term because it is so commonly used by parents and health professionals, but this doesn't mean that we think such children are naughty or deliberately being difficult. Fussy children have problems with food that we need to be able to understand properly if we are to manage their eating behaviour in a helpful way. Fussy children usually have a slightly limited-range diet, but, when asked, parents will report quite a few foods that are eaten. In the first chapters we do therefore give some tips on how best to manage those children who might just be described as 'fussy'.

As we progress through the first part of the book, we then refer more and more to those children who have greater difficulties with food. To begin with, we term these children as being avoidant around food or having a restricted diet. Later we introduce the eating disorder ARFID (Avoidant and Restricted Food Intake Disorder), which describes children and adults who have a very limited-range diet and who have a fearful response to new foods.

Most of this part of the book is written by Gillian Harris, so when I say 'I', I am referring to my own experience, and when I say 'we', I am referring to team clinical practice or team research findings.

The second part of the book focuses exclusively on children with a restricted dietary pattern who would gain a diagnosis of ARFID. This is mainly written by Elizabeth Shea. Here she concentrates on factors that maintain the avoidant response to food and describes approaches to intervention. This part of the book also concentrates on children on the autistic spectrum, who are more likely than neurotypical children to gain a diagnosis of ARFID. Similarly, when she says 'I', she is referring to her own experience, and when she says 'we', she is referring to team clinical practice or team research findings.

Chapter 1

The Early Stages

Why do we eat what we do?

How do babies get to like the foods that they like?

How do they develop the skills that they need to be able to eat?

They sent me home with a baby and no instruction book! I was determined to get it right, though, so I read everything and asked everyone what to do. But when I first gave him food on a spoon, he wouldn't take it; he just spat it out and turned his head. They said to leave it for a while, because he wasn't ready. So I left it, but when I tried again, he still spat the food out. I tried making my own food, I tried buying baby food from the shops, but nothing worked. He even began to scream when he saw the spoon. Eventually, I found one jar of food that he would accept, and we went with that. But when I started to introduce lumps, the same thing happened: he just spat them out and cried. This went on and on. He would take a few foods with his fingers, and then would take some yoghurts, and he didn't mind bread and biscuits. So we got some meals that we could make up. Then when he got to two, he stopped eating some of the few foods that he did eat. I just didn't know what to do anymore. They said leave him to go hungry or just make him eat the food, but I couldn't do that because he got too upset. (Mother of a six-year-old boy)

When we meet a family who want help with their 'fussy' child, the first thing that we want to know is what they were like as baby. How did they respond to food when it was first introduced? This gives us an idea of how and when the problems might have started. Children don't want to be fussy; they are not refusing to eat foods because they are being naughty. They refuse food because they don't like the taste, the texture, or the look of the food; quite often it disgusts them. But this problem with food will have started right back in early infancy; feeding and eating problems start with our first experiences with food.

To begin with, we first have to ask and answer some basic questions. Why do we eat the foods that we eat? How do we get to like them? Why do we get to like them? Why do some people eat practically everything and some people are very fussy? Why is it that some foods are more likely to be rejected than others?

Think of our ancestors, roaming in forests and fields, or by the seashore looking for different things they could eat. When they first moved to a new environment, how did they know what to try and what would be good to eat? Some of the group would have to try a plant or a berry, to see if it would turn out to be safe. Once these adventurous few had found new foods that weren't poisonous in some way, then it would make life easier for others in the group. The others could just copy the eating behaviour of those who had tried the food and were still alive to tell the tale! Learning about which foods to eat is all about learned safety, and we learn about which foods are safe to eat by copying what others eat.

This learning about which foods to eat has to be flexible; humans could not have evolved with fixed food preferences. This is because we live in such a wide range of climates and environments that we have to get our food from many different sources. It would be of little use if we had all evolved to like fish and berries but our family lived in a land-locked desert where these foods are not available. Some foods, however, are more likely to be rejected even though they *are* safe to eat, and this is because they have a strong taste such as bitter, or a difficult texture, maybe slimy or stringy.

Tastes

To understand what is going on here, we need to think first about how we have evolved and how taste preferences change and develop. Babies are born with a preference for a sweet taste; this will lead them to like the taste of breast milk which is slightly sweet and a good energy source. Babies learn to get to like three of the other tastes – salt, sour and umami – quite quickly, because they have got used to these tastes either in breast milk or in complementary solid food, when the baby is introduced to them. The more 'different' tastes that are given during this early stage, the more likely the baby is to accept new tastes. So the tastes or flavours that are usual in foods in any specific cultural group are the tastes that the baby will get to like, as a result of being given them.

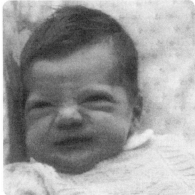

I like sweet; I don't like bitter

So four tastes are easy to get to like, but the last taste – that of bitter – is more difficult. Most mammals, including humans, have evolved with an inborn dislike of a bitter taste, because bitter tastes are usually associated with toxicity (oleander is an example of this – bitter-tasting and deadly poisonous). Plants that have evolved to have a bitter taste even though they might not be poisonous are less likely to be eaten both by mammals and by small children! So the vegetables that we might want our children to eat, such as Brussels sprouts, kale, cabbage and broccoli, are difficult to get to like because of their bitter taste. It takes more tastes to get a liking for these vegetables than it does for vegetables such as carrots, which are quite sweet.

Fussy children's usual food preferences

Sweet tastes are liked from birth	→	chocolate, cakes, biscuits, some fruits and carrots
Salt	↘	→ crisps
Sour	→ taste liking is learned	→ yoghurt, fromage frais
Umami	↗	→ mixed dishes, meat, fish, cheese, tomatoes
Bitter tastes are difficult to learn to like	→	cabbage, broccoli, dark chocolate

Fussy children tend not to eat foods with a bitter taste.

There are also differences in how horrible bitter tastes are found to be. Some children and adults are born with an extreme dislike of bitter tastes; they are bitter 'super tasters'. Others find a bitter taste slightly difficult, and yet some can hardly taste it at all. This means that some children will never get to like Brussels sprouts, however hard you try, and yet a brother or sister in the same family will have no problems with them at all.

There are other taste differences that we are beginning to learn about as well. Some people find the taste of beetroot rather earthy and nasty, some find the taste of coriander rather soapy, and yet others happily eat both beetroot and coriander. There are genetic differences now being discovered in response to many other tastes and foods, such as chamomile, vanilla and even Marmite! So we can't be sure, then, that each of us finds the different tastes of food equally nice; a child who pulls a face at a food that their parent likes might just experience the taste in a different way.

We get to like the tastes of the foods that are safe to eat, because we are given them to eat at an early age, by or around six months. It is often quite easy to get a baby at this early age to accept a new taste. Most babies will take a new taste from a spoon into their mouth without refusing it, or put some finger food in their mouth to try it out. They will accept sweet and slightly sour or slightly salty food quite quickly. But this doesn't happen when the child is older. Older children and adults have to taste a new food about ten times before they get to like it, especially if the new food has a taste that is unusual for them. So with an older fussy child, it isn't easy to get a new food accepted. Some children might agree to try one taste of the food and then say 'I don't like it' and refuse to try the food again. It is not the first taste that is so difficult for many children and parents – it is the second taste!

Maddy had been a vegetarian since the age of 14. She didn't eat meat or fish. Because she had eaten meat as a child, she could touch meat and cook it for her partner, but she did find the smell of the butcher's shop overwhelming and unpleasant. She read everywhere how good it was to have fish in your diet, and so she thought that she would try to start eating some again. But even though she had eaten fish as a child (very reluctantly!), she was unable to actually put any in her mouth. The smell put her off before she started, and she felt totally unable to get the food those last few inches past her lips. With perseverance, she did get a piece of shrimp in; it didn't smell, but she found the texture unpleasant – like chewing rubber. She gave up on the fish after the first taste and decided to stick to a vegetarian diet. The second taste is the most difficult when you are older!

Bitter and slimy!

Basically, we have evolved not to like bitter-tasting green leafy vegetables, and they have evolved a bitter taste to stop mammals like us from eating them. The dislike for green food has nothing much to do with the colour; it is just that green foods tend to be leafy vegetables. Leafy foods also provide very few calories (energy) and their texture is not always pleasant – leafy foods can be very 'stringy'. So although we have evolved to like the foods that are right for our cultural group, often the 'healthy' foods that adults would like children to eat are not always going to be well accepted.

We also seem to have an inborn dislike of certain textures. Slimy-textured foods, such as shellfish or jellied eels are more likely to be refused both by adults and by children. Many children and adults dislike ripe bananas, not just because of the smell but because of the texture. Many are horrified by the idea of a slightly undercooked egg! This is because a slimy texture is once again associated with danger in food. A food that is putrid – that is, rotting – will be slimy and therefore dangerous to eat. And once again some people are more wary of foods of different texture than are others. These difficult textures and tastes then become linked with the smell of the food. People who don't like bananas will often say that they can't cope with the smell, although they were probably first put off eating them by the slimy texture

Smell and sight

The way that a food tastes is very much determined by the way that the food smells. Very little research has been carried out on how reaction to food smells affects children's acceptance and refusal of those foods, but children and adults do tell us that smell can be important in deciding whether or not a food can be eaten. So as tastes combine to give us the unique flavour of a food, so the smell of that food also adds to the mix. Just as babies need to get used to the taste of different foods when these are first introduced to them, they also need to get used to food smells. If foods that are pre-prepared or shop-bought are given to the baby, then there is often no accompanying identifiable smell. We know that babies who are fed home-produced food are more likely to eat a wider range of fruit and vegetables in later childhood than are those who are mainly fed shop-bought food. This could possibly be because the baby does not experience the smell of the food, as well as missing out on the wider range of tastes that come with home-prepared foods. Similarly, when foods are home-prepared, the baby gets used to the way that the food looks, perhaps because they are given a small piece of the food to hold even if the rest of the dish is pureed. Babies need to taste, smell, touch and see the food that is being introduced to them. This is easier if they have experience in all of these senses from around six months.

Responsive feeding

We also have to remember that what we do when we feed our babies will affect them. If we pull a face when we feed a food to our baby, then they will react according to the face that we pull. If we smile and look encouraging, the baby is more likely to try the food that we offer. But we also need to respond to the baby as well. If a baby pulls a face, grimaces or gags when they are fed a new food, then this means they are surprised by the new taste. Usually, if another spoonful of the food is given on the next day, and then the next day, the baby will most probably learn to accept that new taste.

This is not always true, though. Some babies will become very distressed, turn away from the spoon, block their mouth, shut their mouth and then scream. These babies have problems with the taste of the food that you are trying. Is it too bitter? Too sour? With these babies, you might never get the taste accepted easily in early infancy.

One mother didn't like the smell of fish, so when she fed fish pie to her baby, Sarah, she pulled a disgusted face. Sarah, of course, read the signs: 'If she doesn't like it, then neither will I.' Babies respond to our facial expression and tone of voice all the time. The more positive we are when trying something new with them, the more likely they are to be happy trying it once, and then again.

Another mother tried Elliot with broccoli, which he had never had before; he gagged and didn't look as if he liked it. It had a bitter taste. His mother tried the broccoli again the next day, and for the rest of the week offered a little every day while being positive and encouraging. After a week or so he was taking the food quite happily.

So, foods that children easily like the taste of will be those that are sweet. This is because we are born liking the taste of sweet; a sweet taste tells us it is a good source of energy. Children are also more likely to accept those foods that are mildly sour or salty; these are also tastes that are more readily accepted and that we can quickly learn to like. Most 'fussy' children will eat foods like yoghurt or fromage frais (which are slightly sour) and most like milk chocolate, which is sweet (but not dark chocolate, which is bitter). They will often eat some sort of crisps, which are salty. There is also an early preference for fat in foods, so the combination of sugar and fat or salt and fat explains even further why many children and adults like chocolate and crisps! The foods that 'fussy' children are less likely to eat are those that are bitter, such as green vegetables, and foods that have a texture that is stringy, bitty or slimy.

Coping with textures

After this first stage of getting to like the taste of food comes the next stage of getting the baby used to different food textures. This is the time period during which babies must learn the skills to allow them to move food around in the mouth, and to accept the feel of those foods within the mouth. If they don't have lumpy-textured food to eat from about seven months or so, then it becomes increasingly difficult for babies to learn to cope with more solid foods. Parents of children who go on to have a restricted eating pattern usually report that this is the stage – the introduction of textured foods – when they first noticed real difficulties with their babies.

The first stage of accepting tastes is a 'sensitive' stage in development. This is a period in which it is easier for learning to take place; behaviour can still be learned at a later stage, but it is more difficult. So we can learn to like new tastes in later childhood and adulthood, but it takes more time and more effort. This is different from a 'critical' period. This is a time period when a behaviour must be learned, and if this window of opportunity is missed, then the behaviour might never be gained.

This next stage in food acceptance – that of texture acceptance – is a 'critical period'.

In the first year of life babies develop from being able to swallow liquids to being able to chew and swallow harder foods. At the beginning babies hold any liquids on the tongue; this liquid is then swallowed straight over the back of the tongue, without any processing. From around six months or so a baby will be able to mush food on the top of the mouth with the tongue – this is called 'munching'. Then they learn the side-to-side tongue movement necessary to get food from the tongue to the gums and teeth at the side of the mouth. Gradually, as chewing skills develop, the baby can move food from the centre of the mouth to the side of the mouth and back again to the centre. Harder food is broken down at the sides of the mouth; it can then be swallowed in the same way that liquids are swallowed, straight over the back of the tongue.

During this process many babies will get it wrong and try to swallow a lump of food without moving it around the mouth to make it the right size and consistency to swallow. So most babies, when they are learning to eat will cough a little when the food gets to the back of the tongue and the lump is too large to swallow; they may also show a 'gag' response. If a large lump of food is caught on the back of the tongue, it needs to be 'coughed' out to protect the airway. This cough reflex is a safety mechanism to help make sure that what is swallowed is safe; the cough reflex is present from birth.

Mixed foods

The most difficult texture for a baby who is just being introduced to lumpy solids is that found in a mixture of foods. These are usually described as second-stage baby foods and they have small lumps in creamy liquid. It is very difficult to cope with this texture unless the lumps are soft enough to be mushed on the palate at the top of the mouth with the tongue, so that both lumps and soupy base can be swallowed together without triggering the cough or gag response. If the lumps are too hard or too big, then the baby has to try to move the lumps to one side of the mouth and hold them there, while they swallow the creamy base as a liquid. They can then try to process the lumps with a side-to-side tongue movement. This is all quite complex for a baby new to feeding and is more likely to result in the baby trying to swallow the whole lot with a liquid swallow and then triggering the cough or gag response. Most babies will do this a good few times at the beginning of the lumpy solid introduction period, but some babies will find it so uncomfortable that it will put them off trying lumpy food again. 'Fussy' children are most likely to be put off eating lumps because of the way they feel in the mouth.

A good exercise to do to understand how it feels to try to cope with new textures as a baby, or as a child who has very sensitive sides to the mouth, is to try various common foods such as bread, cake, biscuits, cheese, chocolate, crisps, carrot, apple and a lumpy vegetable soup. Hold each food in the centre of your tongue. Remember, you cannot move the food to the side of your mouth. Which foods are easier to process? If you then allow yourself to move the food from side to side, what do you have to do with the lumps in the soup before you can swallow your mouthful?

By the age of 18 months or so, a toddler is able to chew quite difficult foods, such as a piece of apple, without problem. So chewing skills develop throughout infancy into the toddler years and beyond, but the biggest changes occur during the period from six to ten months. This is the age at which babies learn to accept lumpy solid foods in the mouth and to move them with the tongue to the sides of the mouth. If babies are not given, or won't accept, lumpy-textured food in the mouth, then the side-to-side tongue movement is not learned, or learned later but only with great difficulty.

The problem is that if a baby is reluctant to take lumpy-textured foods and coughs or gags and retches, then quite often parents will delay trying lumpy foods, thinking that things will get better as the baby gets older. Unfortunately, it doesn't! If the introduction of lumpy-textured foods is delayed, then the feel of the food in the mouth becomes difficult for the baby.

The insides of the mouth in early infancy are very sensitive to touch. When we are sensitive to something, it feels uncomfortable if anything touches that area. The insides of the mouth only become 'desensitised' as food is moved to the sides of the mouth. If we keep touching an area that is sensitive, then it gradually becomes less uncomfortable when something touches it. Babies only learn the side-to-side tongue movement if they have lumpy solid foods in the mouth which need to be broken down so that they can be swallowed. The sides of the mouth only become used to the feel of food if food is moved by the tongue from the centre to the sides of the mouth

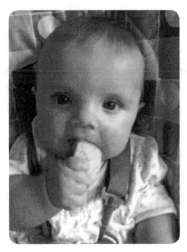

Learning to cope with textures

Easier textures

Some foods are easier for babies to accept than others. There are foods that can be held in the mouth and do not need to be moved from side to side in order to be swallowed. They do not need to be chewed. These foods are called bite-and-melt or bite-and-dissolve foods. If small pieces of bite-and-melt foods are held on the tongue, then they turn into liquid with the heat of the body and can be swallowed using a liquid swallow. If small pieces of bite-and-dissolve foods are held on the tongue, then they will be broken down by the saliva, so that they can also be taken down using a liquid swallow, straight over the back of the tongue. These foods are the easiest introduction to solid foods. They get the child used to the feel of textured foods at least on and around the tongue. These are the textures we would start with when trying to help with a child who cannot cope with solid foods in the mouth but who will only accept liquids or smooth purees and yoghurts. So the easiest food textures for a baby to cope with are yoghurts and custards, soft biscuits, soft crisps and milk chocolate. Of course, these are the foods that have easier tastes as well!

Table 1.1 The progression of textured foods

Food	Description	Example
Smooth puree	Quite runny or smooth with no lumps	Pureed stewed fruit Pureed stewed vegetables Weetabix soaked in milk or fruit juice Fromage frais Smooth yoghurt
Soft mash	Fairly smooth with small soft lumps. It is mashed with a fork rather than liquidised	Banana mashed with a fork Mashed potato Mashed baked beans Scrambled eggs Steamed fish Dhal – well-cooked lentils
Bite-and-dissolve finger foods	These dissolve in the mouth and do not need any chewing but do need enough control to hold food in the mouth until it dissolves	Wotsits Skips Quavers Pom-Bear teddies Weeny Wotsits Monster Munch Pink wafer biscuits Ice cream wafers Most sponge fingers Rice cakes
Bite-and-melt finger foods	These melt in the mouth, similar to bite-and-dissolve but coat the mouth more	Maltesers cut into quarters Chocolate buttons

cont.

Food	Description	Example
Bite-and-soft-chew foods	These need some preparation or munching in the mouth before being swallowed	Very ripe peeled fruit – e.g. pear, melon, avocado, peeled grapes cut in half
		Soft pieces of cooked potato, sweet potato, carrot, beetroot, soft chips, cooked florets of cauliflower, broccoli
		Mini pasta shapes
		Soft biscuits – e.g. malted milk, Rich Tea, digestive biscuits
		Sandwiches made with soft white bread (crusts cut off) and smooth fillings – e.g. cheese spread, butter and Marmite, hummus
		Soft cake – e.g. Madeira cake
		Pancakes
		Cheese triangles, cubes of soft cheese
		Small pieces of well-cooked fish, corned beef
		Fishcakes (you need to take the coating off)
Bite-and-splinter foods	Need a little more chewing before being swallowed	Bread sticks
		Cream crackers
		Crisps
		Poppadoms
		Ryvita
		Hula Hoops

Bite-and-lump foods	These need good chewing skills and are usually the last foods to be mastered by most children	Raw apple Chicken nuggets Whole grapes Crusty bread Pizza Sausages

Problems with textures

Some older babies – those who are more sensitive to touch – will become more and more reluctant to take any textured foods into their mouth the older they get, if they haven't accepted textured foods in the first year. They may be more reluctant than other babies to take any textured foods when they are first introduced. These sensory-sensitive babies sometimes get into their second year not taking any foods that don't have a pureed, creamy, bite-and-melt or bite-and-dissolve texture. Babies who are so sensory-sensitive in the mouth that they cannot take a full range of textured foods are usually termed 'orally defensive'; they are 'defending' their mouth from a very uncomfortable experience. They may also have had more problems coping with lumpy-textured foods in the mouth when they were first introduced. They can often vomit when they cough to clear the food from the tongue. Babies who have reflux are more likely to cough and vomit when they try to cope with lumpy-textured foods.

Summary

- As many new tastes as possible should be introduced when first starting with foods. It takes fewer tastes in early infancy to get a preference for that taste or that food.

- As children get older, it takes more tastes to get to like a food. One taste will not do it!

- Some babies have an inborn dislike of certain tastes which makes it difficult for them to accept some tastes, such as that of bitter foods.

- Babies will pick up on the facial expression of whoever is feeding them new foods.

- Foods with a more solid texture should be introduced from around six months. The baby has to learn the oral-motor skills that are needed to process solids food around the mouth. If the baby doesn't get the experience of solid-textured foods within the first year, then they are likely to become orally defensive, to dislike and refuse textured foods in their mouth.

- Sensory-sensitive babies are likely to dislike the feeling of textured foods in their mouth, and have more problems processing lumpy-textured food.

- Most children who go on to have a restricted diet are reported by their parents as refusing textured foods when these were first introduced.

. . .

Tips for parents and carers

- Give as many different food tastes as possible, as early as possible in the feeding process.
  - o Even if your baby makes a face when you try a new taste, do offer it again; gradually, your baby will get used to it.
- Get your baby used to the smell of the food that you are feeding them; cook food for them yourself whenever possible.
- Give your baby soft pieces of food to hold at mealtimes from around six months.
  - o Your baby will get used to the feel of food in their hands and around their face. This will also get them used to the look of the food that you are feeding to them.
- Get different textured food into the diet as soon as you can after six months.

o The inside of the mouth is only desensitised if textured food goes in and around it. Oral-motor skills are only learned if the baby has experience of textured foods.

- Let your baby get messy! Babies who are allowed to get messy at mealtimes are more likely to try new foods. Let them put their fingers in the food that you are giving them and paint the high chair with it!

. . .

Chapter 2

Neophobia
The Onset of the Fear of New and Different Foods

Where are we are up to now?

In the first year it is quite easy to introduce new tastes and textures, if these are introduced early enough at the appropriate time. There are inborn differences, however, between babies with regard to taste and texture acceptance; some babies will react more strongly than others. If the introduction of solid-textured foods is delayed, then the baby will be more likely to have problems accepting and processing textured foods as they move into the second year. Those babies who might be described as sensory-sensitive are more likely to be reluctant to try textured foods.

The second year

It might seem to be quite easy to get babies and children to accept new foods in the first years of life. Some will have had a few problems with tastes perhaps, and a few problems with accepting textures, but this is nothing compared with the food refusal that starts at around the age of two years. This stage is sometimes a surprise for parents; suddenly, children will look at a food and refuse it on sight. It could be a new food, or sometimes a food that they have had before but this time something about it has changed. This period is described as the neophobic stage – the fear of the new; but it is also the fear of the different.

The fear response

In earlier infancy there will have been other times when a baby's behaviour will suddenly change because something is not quite right.

The 'fear of strangers' occurs for most babies at around nine months. They might have been okay with new faces up until this time, but suddenly, if the new person doesn't quite look right, then the fear response kicks in; the infant becomes clingy and wary. One of my daughters showed a sudden fear of a colleague with a beard, because she hadn't met anyone with a beard before, and so they looked unusual to her. Toddlers will be wary of anyone who looks slightly different from those they are used to, or who doesn't behave in the way that they expect. After the 'fear of strangers' stage comes the fear of new toys; another of my children was suddenly terrified of a Jack-in-the-box.

All children go through a process during which they get used to people, toys and food, and then become fearful of any example that doesn't look quite right. This doesn't just happen with humans – it happens with other mammals as well – so it isn't about a child being naughty or learning to be defiant. It is learning to be wary of something that doesn't look as expected and that could possibly be harmful; the difference signals danger. It is important, then, that a child refuses the food without tasting it. If a new or slightly different food doesn't look right, then it could possibly be poisonous. We have evolved not to try new foods without some thought.

Fear is processed by a part of the brain called the amygdala. The reaction of this part of the brain to something that we fear is pre-conscious; we react before we are aware that we have seen, smelt, heard or touched the thing that we fear. When the brain is first aware of something that we fear, it starts up the 'fight or flight response'; the body gets ready to run, produces adrenalin and shuts down the digestive process. Frightened children are not in a state to try new foods! Another part of the brain has to come into action to help us control our fears – the prefrontal cortex. With young children we have to wait until they are old enough to reason it through and work to conquer their fears.

Most adults will show a fear-type response if they are faced with a food that they have never had before and that looks nothing like any food they have ever experienced. To a greater or lesser degree they will look carefully at the food, they might smell it, they might poke it with a fork, but what will make them eat it? Well, they are more likely to eat it if others around are eating it without coming to any obvious harm and seeming to enjoy it. We learn if food is safe by watching others around us: if they eat a food and they are okay, then the food is probably safe to eat. Adults are not usually forced to eat a new food – they can eat it or not depending on how happy they feel about trying it, and they will usually just try a small piece to see what the taste and texture is like before committing to a larger mouthful. Children will do the same; they are more likely to try a new food if they see another adult, or other children, eat it, and if they are allowed just to eat a small piece without being pushed into trying it.

There are also differences between adults and children in how strong the neophobic response is. Some will be very wary of new foods, others more willing to try. There are even adults out there who say that they will try any food at all – even animal road kill. This difference between people is an example of genetic diversity: there have to be some of us that will try new foods without worry and some who would be very careful about trying a food that looks even slightly different. Remember, if early humans were faced with a new environment in which they didn't know which plants or berries were safe to eat, then it would be useful to have people who would try anything and possibly die in the process, and those who would hold back to see who didn't die. Those who held back would copy the eating habits of those who lived to tell the tale. Perhaps the 'fussy' eaters will always survive!

We know that there are individual differences in how strong the neophobic response is, and that children who are more neophobic are likely to be more fussy and anxious. We also know that there is a family link: neophobic children are more likely to have neophobic parents. This can be because their parents are genetically determined to be neophobic. Or sometimes a fussy parent can signal to their toddler that they too don't like trying new foods. This doesn't mean, though, that extreme neophobia in the child is always the fault of the parent and because the child has copied their 'fussy' behaviour.

Understanding the neophobic response

We can see that the neophobic response is something to do with the way in which the child sees the food by thinking about the 'fear of the different' response. Many toddlers will suddenly refuse a meal or a food that they have eaten before, and they are more likely to refuse 'mixed' foods. A recipe where the foods are combined in some way is more likely to be refused because it is more likely than a single food to look different on subsequent presentations.

Someone added green bits to my pasta bake!

Why is this? What is going on here? The reason behind this is that the toddler is coming to the age at which they are beginning to form food categories, and this is why it is a 'fear of the different' rather than 'fear of the new'. Foods are refused because they don't exactly match an internal visual image of a known food (a prototype). Children at this age are concentrating on the exact details of each food rather than on general factors that the foods might have in common. So a food that they are given that they usually eat must look precisely the same, down to the last detail. Toast must be the exact shade of brown, biscuits must be whole and with the usual writing on them, crisps can't be curly, and chips must not have burnt ends. The exact detail shows that the food is safe, because the food has to match the internal prototype.

This is a biscuit; this is not a biscuit!

This, of course, applies to packets as well. The outside appearance of a food tells us whether the food is safe to eat or not. A 'safe' apple might have to be a red apple rather than a green one. If we give a child a food from a packet, then the packet is the thing that tells us about the safety of the food, and that means that the packet, just like the outside appearance of a food, must stay the same. If the packet changes because it has a 'money off' sticker or Christmas decorations, or the manufacturers just decide to update it, then the packet no longer looks exactly the same and the food might no longer be safe to eat. This often gives the parents problems when a food package of one of the few foods eaten by their child is changed; many parents find themselves scouting around distant supermarkets to stock up on 'old-style' food and packaging.

One of the few foods William would eat was a chocolate bar in a paper wrapper. The manufacturers decided to update this to a silver foil wrapper. It took a lot of effort on the mother's part (luckily, she was warned in advance) to show her son that chocolate coming out of the old wrapper was the same as the chocolate coming out of the new wrapper, but she succeeded. Richard's mother knew that he would eat chips from McDonald's™, so she took some cartons home from McDonald's™ and put home cooked French fries in the McDonald's™ carton. They didn't look quite right, of course, and were refused, so this strategy failed!

Children also have preferences for different flavours of their favourite foods: strawberry yoghurt rather than blackcurrant, cheese and onion crisps rather than salt and vinegar. The colour of the packet also usually tells you about the flavour of the food inside, so children will attend closely to the small detail on the packet to be sure that it is the usual food with the correct flavour.

The neophobic response can also be seen when the taste or texture of a food has been changed, even though the food might look the same. The child might eat some of the food if they think it looks right but refuse a second taste or spit the food out when they actually taste it. Once these foods have been refused after the first taste, the food might never be accepted again.

Kevin would eat normal bread as part of his daily diet, but on advice his mother decided to try a gluten-free diet. She offered Kevin his normal meal with plain bread, and it did look the same. He tasted the bread, could tell the difference in taste and texture, refused it and would never again accept it. It is never a good idea to start an exclusion diet with a child who has a restricted intake unless there are good medical reasons.

Why lots of biscuits and no vegetables?

Most children grow out of the neophobic response by the age of five years or so. Many will happily try a new food, especially if they have seen others eat it either at home or at school, or when at their friends' houses. Some foods, however, will be more difficult to accept than others. Foods that look familiar are more likely to be tried. Even some very 'fussy' children will try another example of a known food if it looks very similar. Most parents know that their children will happily accept a new kind of biscuit or a new kind of cake, but they are less likely to try a new vegetable. This is because most biscuits look very similar, but vegetables look very different from each other.

These biscuits look very much the same; the vegetables are all different colours and shapes

Often the texture of a vegetable also looks 'difficult', whereas the texture of a biscuit looks easy and consistent. We can look at a food and, quite surprisingly, tell from just looking at it what the texture of the food will seem like in our mouth. When we see a new type of biscuit, it is likely to be a similar shape and colour to biscuits that we have had in the past. The texture will also look the same. Biscuits tend to be brown or beige and dry and crumbly, so we are better able to predict the mouth feel; we know what that food will be like in our mouth.

As children are gradually beginning to form categories and to make generalisations as they grow a little older, they can make predictions:

- 'That food looks more or less the same as a food I have had before.'

- 'I think I know what it will feel like in my mouth.'

- 'It has the same word label (biscuit) so I guess it will be safe to eat.'

Vegetables don't fit into this pattern of reasoning, though. Each vegetable more or less differs from every other vegetable in size, colour and perceived texture. And yet we call them all vegetables! It is then very difficult for a child to be sure that this new example of a vegetable is 'safe' to eat; it looks so different.

Moving on from the neophobic response

Children gradually move out of the neophobic stage but only if they are *able* to imitate other people, and if they *want* to imitate other people, in their eating behaviour and food choices. Most children will watch others eat; either family members or other children at nursery or pre-school playgroup. Then – because they want to imitate and be like their classmates – they will try the foods that the others are eating. Children will copy cartoon characters, characters that they see on TV or in books; when they want to 'be like' someone, they are more likely to copy them. Also, as children get older, they are able to see similarities between foods that have the same 'label', so one type of bread is likely to taste almost the same as any other bread, and is therefore safe to try.

But this progression is only seen in children who want to imitate others, who can imitate others and who can see the similarities between foods with the same 'label'. Children with restricted diets, especially if they are on the autistic spectrum, don't always imitate others and can't make generalisations across foods.

The mother of one girl with a restricted diet suggested that she try a certain new food, saying that her best friend ate it. Bethan said, 'Why should I do something just because she does it?' Her mother was stumped for an answer! Some children just don't see the need to imitate others. When Daniel took his packed lunch to school, his parents hoped he might eventually change what was in it to be more like the other children. Daniel didn't change his packed lunch at all, but the other children started to change their packed lunches so that theirs was more like Daniel's rather odd combination of foods.

Children will also taste new foods if they are prompted to touch them, either when helping with food preparation or when touching foods in play. Touching will help, but even just seeing the food, or a picture or photo of the food, will also help in getting the child to try the new food. These strategies work better, though, with children who are not very fussy. 'Fussy' children have a greater fear of trying new foods, and the greater the fear of trying new a food, the less likely the child is to want to touch new foods, or to imitate what someone else is eating.

One study shows that if pre-school children were given pieces of fruit or vegetables that they didn't usually eat, and were asked to use these pieces to copy and make a picture of a caterpillar, then they were more likely to try a new food afterwards. So just touching and smelling and seeing a new food lessens the neophobic response. Although very neophobic children are often reluctant to touch new foods, we have found that playing a game with the child that distracts them from the food will get them to touch it even if the food is sticky or dusty. So we would perhaps have a competition with the child to see who could get most chocolate buttons into a container – luckily, the child often doesn't notice that their hands are getting sticky with chocolate!

Why are some children more neophobic than others?

The neophobic response is stronger in those children who are sensory-hypersensitive – that is, those children who react more strongly to stimuli around them in the environment (see Chapter 3). This is because children who react more strongly to the environment around them pay more attention to the small 'local' detail of objects and have more problems seeing the wider picture; they are less likely to see the general properties that objects have in common. This is especially true of children who are visually hypersensitive. These sensory-sensitive children attend much more than others to small differences that they can see, between a food that they know and a new food. A biscuit from one shop might be accepted but the same biscuit from another shop rejected because the writing on it is not the same. The more they attend to the small differences, the more likely they are to refuse the new food as different. We know that children who are rated as 'fussy' eaters tend to be more sensory-sensitive. So an extreme neophobic response is usually linked to sensory hypersensitivity.

These biscuits are not the same; they have different writing on them

Children who are 'fussy' also tend to be more anxious, especially around food. This anxiety increases hypervigilance – that is, attention to small details in the environment that might be important in signalling danger. So the more anxious a child becomes around mealtimes or around food, the more they will attend to those small, usually irrelevant, details of the food in front of them. They will make the decision that there is a difference between their known foods and this different food; the food will then be refused because it is not safe to eat. If 'fussy' children or restricted eaters are forced to eat food or made anxious around food or mealtimes, they are less likely to eat.

This anxiety can be provoked in some unexpected ways. Stewart, 14 years old, went to a hotel with his parents. They thought that the buffet-style meals provided would give him the choice of foods that he needed in order to find something he could eat. But the anxiety about having to make a choice from so many foods, while the pressure was on him to choose, meant that he couldn't decide on anything. He had to go back to his table and get his mother to choose for him.

Forcing, prompting, bribing and hiding

We know that copying others' eating habits and touching and seeing new foods all help children to move on from the neophobic stage, but what of other strategies? Can parents be firm and insist a food is eaten? Can they prompt and suggest? Can they hide a new food in an accepted dish? We know that any kind of force or coercion will lead to higher levels of fear and anxiety and so reduce appetite. Even insisting that a child sits in front of a new food is very unlikely to get a 'fussy' or avoidant child to eat it. It will just make them more anxious around mealtimes. Prompting and pleading don't work either if the prompting is seen by the child as putting any kind of pressure on them to do something that they don't want to do, and are afraid of doing. If 'fussy' or avoidant children are to try a new food, they need to be calm, and to be with someone or in a situation where others are calm; only then are they likely to try the food.

In one study which we carried out (Blissett *et al.* 2016) parents were asked to prompt their child to eat a new food, or to model eating a new food, or to do both. Children rated as 'fussy' eaters were less likely to try the new food if their parent prompted them to do so. Children who were not fussy would eat if prompted. Both groups of children were more likely to try the new food if their parent modelled eating it. So prompting might work for some children, but not for the group of 'fussy' or avoidant eaters

Many parents try rewarding a child for eating a new food; most parents call this bribing! This can work but only if it is done in a certain way, and we use this technique in Part 2 of the book. What doesn't work is when one food is used as a reward for eating another: 'Eat up your vegetables, and then you can have some pudding.' This just makes the child think that pudding is nice because all rewards are nice and that vegetables are nasty because tasks are unlikely to be pleasant. Parents also might try to offer a reward to a child if they eat a new meal at a family mealtime, or eat a new food that the child finds really disgusting.

Sometimes there is just no reward high enough that would make the child try the food!

It is often suggested that a good way to get a child to eat a new food is to 'hide' it in another food. So you could chop a new vegetable up into small pieces and hide it in the pasta that the child already eats. We think about this tactic again in the next chapter, but with a 'fussy' child it is not a good strategy. New food is rejected on sight; sensory-sensitive children tend to be sensitive to small details especially in and around food, and can also detect small changes in taste. So although parents might get away with hiding a food with a child who isn't very fussy, they are unlikely to get away with hiding a food from a 'fussy' child. At best the child will fish all of the pieces out of the meal; at worst the child will refuse that entire meal when it is offered again – it is no longer the same, it is different.

Holly's mother tried to cut up mushrooms very small and add them to her mixed vegetables. Holly found every piece of mushroom, however small, and left it on the side of her plate.

Jane would eat baby porridge as one of the two foods that she would accept. A health professional suggested that her parents add some pureed fruit to the porridge. She took one spoonful, and refused to eat porridge again. That food was lost from her diet.

Children with restricted eating patterns

Children who continue with very restricted diets don't grow out of the neophobic stage as other children do. As these children continue with their fear of the new and their fear of the different, more and more foods are lost from their diet with every small change in presentation, production and packaging. These children remain very 'brand-loyal'; they will only eat certain foods, specific brands and perhaps only one flavour. And as these children get older, they do not imitate those around them in their eating habits.

As others around them feel more stress at the very limited range of foods that the child will eat, so anxiety around food and mealtimes increases, and the child's ability to move on decreases. Children at this age, around three or four years, also do not see that there is any need to change what they eat. They are usually quite happy with their restricted and safe diet. They are not aware of health implications or how inconvenient their limited choice of foods will be as they get older. They are also not aware of their parents' anxiety about what they won't eat. So when we think of interventions for children with a severely restricted diet, we need to remember that we are coping with a fear response and a response that the child has no motivation to change in the early years.

The age of neophobia is linked to the cognitive age rather than the actual age of the child. We have noticed that children with developmental delay often don't show the neophobic response until they achieve the appropriate cognitive stage – usually when they start to acquire language. So a child might eat very well until perhaps the age of five when they start to produce their first words, and at this age suddenly start to refuse to eat.

Desire for sameness

The neophobia response means that avoidant children keep to a diet that is rigidly the same every day, and sometimes every meal. This seems similar to the 'desire for sameness' observed in many on the autistic spectrum. Are the two things the same? Food has to be the same, and to look the same, because otherwise the child cannot predict what the food will taste and feel like in the mouth. Those on the autistic spectrum like to keep to the same routines and rituals, and can get very upset if things change. So the general 'desire for sameness' is similar to that seen in avoidant eating, but with food there is a primitive 'learned safety' rule that makes the behaviour more difficult to change: 'If this food isn't the same as the food that I usually eat, it might poison me or it might make me sick.' The inability to move on to foods that look different is a stronger and more universal response than is the 'desire for sameness'. But there might be one general 'desire for sameness' that children with avoidant eating do show and that is for eating utensils or cutlery, perhaps because they predict the food that comes on them.

A call from a nurse on the ward at the children's hospital was to ask for help with an eight-month-old baby who had suddenly stopped taking her food from a spoon (the only texture she could take). When we talked about what had happened before Sally started to refuse her food, we realised that the nurses had been giving Sally her bitter-tasting medicine on a spoon of the same colour as the one that was used to feed her. Sally could no longer tell whether the spoon would give her something that tasted awful or something that tasted nice. A change of spoon colour for the medicine solved the problem.

Failure in early learning?

In some cases, the child will have a limited-range diet and be very reluctant to try new foods in the toddler period just because they have not been given enough different tastes and textures in their first year. If they have not experienced many tastes and textures, then the baby will have a limited range of foods that they accept, not because they are avoidant, but just because they have not learned to like a range of tastes and textures.

Summary

- The neophobic response – the fear of new or different foods – usually starts at around two years.

- Food that looks different will be rejected on sight and without tasting.

- This response is thought to be of evolutionary benefit.
- The response is linked to the cognitive stage – when children are beginning learn about food categories.
- Children who are anxious and sensory-sensitive are more likely to be highly neophobic.
- Most children develop out of the neophobic response from about five years.
- Most children from about five years will imitate the eating habits of friends and family.
- Avoidant children with a limited diet:
  - stay in the neophobic stage, and their diet becomes increasingly more restricted
  - pay attention to the small local details of the foods that they eat, and are brand- and packaging-'loyal'
  - are not motivated to change and do not see the need to imitate others.

. . .

Tips for parents and carers

Neophobia is a normal developmental stage so:

Don't

- Panic! Very few neophobic children have health problems because of their limited-range diet.
- Prompt. This makes a 'fussy' child less likely to try a new food.
- Coerce. This will make a 'fussy' child feel more anxious.
- Bribe. If they are fearful about eating it, a bribe won't help.
- Hide. If they find the new food, they might never eat the safe food again.

Do

- Allow them to eat the foods that they like.
- Model eating new foods in front of the child.
- Play games with your child that:
  - are fun
  - involve them in touching, seeing and smelling new foods
  - distract them from the foods with which they are playing.

. . .

Chapter 3

Sensory Factors and How These Affect Food Acceptance

Where have we got to?

In the first year of life it is quite easy to get babies to try new foods, although there are differences between babies in their responses to both tastes and textures. Then, at around two years, the neophobic response begins; this is a fear of new or different foods. It is thought to be of evolutionary benefit; foods which might possibly be poisonous, because they differ from food usually eaten, are rejected on sight. Children at this age are attending to the small 'local' details of the food that they are eating. These local details give them information about whether or not the food is safe to eat. Any food which differs slightly from the norm – burnt toast, broken biscuits – will be refused. Children who are more anxious than others and who are more sensory-sensitive are more likely to have a strong neophobic response. Most children start to grow out of the neophobic stage from around five years, when they begin to be able to form better general food categories – that is, 'I like this bread so I will like that bread too; all bread will taste the same.' At this age they are also happier to copy the eating habits of those around them. Children with a restricted diet, however, stay in the neophobic stage. They stick to their known foods. For them, 'learned safety' is dependent upon the small details of packaging and presentation that they attend to on known foods. These children are likely to be too anxious to move on and try new foods.

The sensory-sensitive baby!

What is sensory sensitivity?

We all feel and react to our environment through our sensory systems. We have seven of these.

We have a sense of hearing, a sense of seeing or of sight (the visual system), a sense of balance, a sense of where our body is in space and, most importantly for learning about food, we have senses of taste, smell and touch. These senses give us information about the world around us, and allow us to react to the incoming information in a way that directs our behaviour. If we smell burning, we might run towards the fire to put it out or run away from the fire to escape.

An eighth sense is also now being described – that of interoception. This is the sense that enables us to be aware of our bodily states, such as hunger, thirst, fullness, body temperature, pain and nausea. It is also suggested that this sense enables us to be fully aware of the emotions that we are currently experiencing. Children and adults who have a restricted diet, and those on the autistic spectrum, often have problems with this self-awareness of internal states.

The information from these senses travels to the brain to help us to navigate the world around us, but much of the information is not picked up by our central processing system. We pick and choose what we attend to and only attend to those bits of information that are important for us at the time. A lot of what is around us is ignored.

There are differences between people in how reactive they are to information coming to their brains through these sensory systems. Some children and adults are very aware of a smell, a touch or a taste, and some children and adults hardly react at all to this incoming information. Some will find the smell of public toilets so overwhelming that they cannot use them; others will hardly notice the smell at all. An overreaction to sensory input is termed sensory hypersensitivity; an under-reaction is termed sensory hyposensitivity. These differences in reaction to sensory input seem to be inborn, but early experience can also make babies and children more reactive to sensory input. Children and babies who suffer from reflux or have to have surgery in and around the mouth are more likely to be sensory-hypersensitive.

We also react differently to what is around us if we are very stressed or anxious. Anxiety makes us hypervigilant. We start to attend to the environment and the things in it quite differently; we notice small details in the objects close to us. If we are stressed or anxious, we are on the look-out for danger so that we can react appropriately. The stress hormones produced in times of danger prepare us for 'fight or flight', and if we are going to do either of these, then we need to be very aware of anything in our immediate environment which might be relevant to the threat being posed.

At the dentist, or just as they start your anaesthetic before an operation, you are likely to feel anxious about what is going to happen; you try to look around to take in all the details of the equipment around you. Is there anything that looks really awful? What are they going to do with that needle? Anxiety makes you hypervigilant; you attend to all that is going on. You don't filter out details as we usually do. This reaction has a survival benefit: when you can get up and run, you know where the door is!

Sensory hypersensitivity can affect feeding and eating behaviours in many ways

Some babies will find it more difficult to accept new tastes from a spoon when these are first offered. Sensory-sensitive babies are more likely to react to different tastes when these are offered. This is most likely to happen if these babies have been offered too few foods, too late in the period of introduction of foods, at or around six months.

Smell is also very much part of how we get the flavour of a food. So babies who might not like the taste of a new food will begin to turn their head away before the spoon comes to their mouth, because they react to the smell. In later childhood, the taste of a disliked food is quickly signalled by the smell, and the smell itself becomes aversive.

As new textures of foods are offered to the baby at around the age of six months or so, then sensory-hypersensitive babies will find the feel of different textures within the mouth more uncomfortable than do other babies.

This age – that of the introduction of lumps – is the age at which most parents report that problems with their very 'fussy' child first began. Parents report that the baby would often spit the lumpy food out when it was first offered and then cry if it was offered again. The baby would also be more likely to try to swallow the lumpy-textured food whole, rather than trying to move it around the mouth; this would mean that they would be more likely to gag on the lumps.

The insides of the mouth are sensitive to touch in all babies, but more so in those who are sensory-sensitive. So these babies try to keep food in the centre of the mouth and avoid moving the food to the more sensitive sides of the mouth. This means that they have to process the food with a liquid swallow, straight over the back of the tongue with no side-to-side processing. A gag response is then triggered as the lump of food hits the back of the tongue. Sometimes, if the baby finds this very uncomfortable, they retch and can follow this with a vomit, to clear the unpleasant lump of food from the back of the mouth.

The whole process is so unpleasant for the baby that they often avoid solid-textured food when it is next offered. These babies then 'fail' to move on to lumpy-textured solids and quite often still only eat soft-textured foods (yoghurts or first-stage commercial baby foods) well into the second year.

One way of working out if your child is sensitive in the sides of the mouth is whether or not they will allow you to clean their teeth to the side. Many sensitive children are happy to have the front teeth brushed, but refuse when the toothbrush goes further in and round to the side teeth. Children who don't like the toothbrush in the sides of the mouth will also be reluctant to hold food there.

When finger foods are introduced, the sensory-sensitive baby is also less likely to want to pick the food up or touch the food at all. Most babies want to grab at the food that they are being fed, they want to hold the spoon, they want to get some food in their hand and to squash and mush it into their face if they can't find their mouth. Not so for sensory-sensitive babies. They don't like mess; they don't like getting their fingers messy or their face messy. Other babies will stick their hand in the yoghurt and draw pictures on their tray, but not the sensory-hypersensitive baby: they keep their hands clean at all times.

I like to play with my food!

Messy play is still very important for sensory-sensitive children. This is the way to 'desensitise' them to the feel of different textures on their hands. Dry textures are easy for most children to touch; it is sticky wet textures that are most difficult. It is also a good idea to allow the baby to get messy around the face and mouth; this will help them in later infancy to allow the feel of foods on the lips. Some sensory-sensitive toddlers will not feed themselves from a spoon because they are worried that they will get sticky food on their lips; they insist on parents feeding them well into childhood.

Difficult and easy textures

Specific textures are more difficult for sensory-hypersensitive babies and children. Slimy textures often seem to pose a problem. Many adults can't cope with slimy foods, such as bananas or shell- fish; this is because slimy textures can have an unpleasant feel in the mouth. Anything that needs a lot of chewing at the sides of the mouth also poses problems. Meat in its original form (rather than processed meats such as chicken nuggets) is usually found difficult and refused. Mixed textures are difficult – the lumps in a mixed-textured dish have to be moved to the side of the mouth while the runnier part of the meal has to be swallowed with a liquid swallow (some second-stage commercial baby foods are refused for this reason). Anything too 'dusty' or 'chewy' can also be quickly refused because of the feel of the food in the mouth and on the fingers. This leaves most sensory-sensitive children and adults with a limited range of textures that they will accept. This is usually called the brown/beige carbohydrate diet!

Foods that are accepted have a common dry, uniform, easily processed texture, such as bread, soft crisps, dry cereals, processed meats or potatoes (fish fingers, turkey shapes, potato faces). In addition to this, yoghurts or custards which are totally smooth, with absolutely no lumps, might also be accepted. But these have to be eaten without touching the lips or around the mouth. Usually, some form of chocolate is accepted, this is because chocolate melts in the mouth and so doesn't leave a 'lump' that has to be processed by moving the food to the sides of the mouth. Similarly, bite-and-dissolve foods – those that break down quickly in the saliva on the tongue – are a popular texture with sensory-hypersensitive children.

Smell, sound and sight

So, sensory-sensitive children are likely to only accept a limited range of tastes and textures, but there will also be other problems around food and eating. Some children can tell that a new food that they haven't tasted before is different according to the smell of the food, and will refuse it on that basis. Children who are sensory-sensitive also often find the smell of other people's food disgusting. This means that they cannot easily sit at a meal table while their family eat or sit in the dining hall at school while other children eat. These children find it uncomfortable to go in the kitchen when food is being prepared, or go into shops where there is a strong food smell. Other smells will also bother them; they may be sensitive to toilet smells, for example, and dislike using toilets away from home.

Further problems might also crop up with children who are sensory-sensitive. They are more likely to be sensitive to noise. Quite often they cannot filter out background noises and attend to the one thing that they should be listening to. The background noise can be a distraction which stops them from concentrating on the task in hand. This can be a big problem for children at school. Or it could be that the noise is uncomfortable for them and overwhelming. This means that, once again, school dining rooms can be a problem: the noise is a constant cacophony that cannot either be filtered out or attended to. The same might be true of cafés, restaurants, supermarkets and stations.

Elliot was taken to a Christmas pantomime at a very small theatre. He is sensitive to noise. One of the performers came on to the stage and started to shout rather loudly. This was so uncomfortable that Elliot had to be taken out.

Another little girl, Becky, had a birthday celebration arranged for her, but someone brought balloons, which the other children burst. That was the end of the birthday celebration!

There can also be problems with the visual system. Most of us only attend to those things in the visual world that we need to be aware of. A lot of detail is ignored because the visual system is not passing those details on to the other parts of the brain in order to trigger a response. But children and adults who are visually hypersensitive can be distracted by small details in the world around them that others of us do not 'see', because we do not attend to them. They might be distracted by dust particles floating in the light, a pattern on a chair seat. Because they cannot stop themselves from attending to small detail, and their visual system is not ignoring these small distracters, they are not able to attend to the bigger picture. It is really a case of not seeing the wood for the trees. This difficulty might not seem to be important when thinking about what we eat and which foods we choose to eat, but we will see in later chapters that it is really the key to the whole problem of restricted and avoidant eating.

When I asked Charlie what the chairs in my clinic room had in common – they all have legs, backs, seats – he looked at the material covering one chair and said that it had a very small diamond pattern in the material (the others did not), so all the chairs were different. Usually, a child of Charlie's age (eight years) would see what they all had in common rather than concentrate on this 'irrelevant' detail. He missed out on the fact that you could sit on each of them.

Hyposensitivity

At the other end of the spectrum from hypersensitivity is sensory hyposensitivity. This means that sensory input is not responded to, rather than overreacted to. Children who are hyposensitive to taste, smell and touch can often overeat, rather than be wary about what they eat. These children will also seek out stimulation within the environment rather than avoid it. Strangely perhaps, children can be hypersensitive in some areas and yet hyposensitive in other areas. So although sensory-hypersensitive children might overreact to tastes, smell, touch and sound, they might not notice pain or respond to temperature. One big problem might be that they don't always seem to feel hunger, so they do not have good interoceptive responses. However, this lack of a feeling of hunger can sometimes be because children who are restricted and avoidant around food find the whole process of eating so stressful that they are put off eating. Their dislike of food means that the process is, for them, not enjoyable and best avoided.

There are, of course, children who are hyposensitive in all domains. These children are more likely to eat anything, to accept new tastes quickly and not to have problems with different textures. But they also tend to stuff their mouth too full, or try to take other children's food, and they are not aware when they have enough to eat. These children pose a different problem for parents. It is difficult to get them to keep their weight at a reasonable level because they will eat any food that is around, and still want more. In a school that I visited, a hyposensitive boy liked to sit next to an avoidant boy, because he could finish off all the food on his plate that he did not want!

Autism and sensory sensitivity

Sensory disorders are more likely to be seen in children on the autistic spectrum. This means that eating disorders related to sensory hypersensitivity or sensory hyposensitivity are also more likely to be seen in children on the autistic spectrum. Many children who are reported by their parents as having very restricted diets in late infancy will go on to gain a diagnosis, often of high-functioning autism or Asperger's syndrome. But there will also be children who would not receive a diagnosis, even though they might have some traits suggestive of autism, and have a very restricted diet. These children do, however, have one thing in common with the children who do get a diagnosis of autism: they are sensory-hypersensitive. We have found that all children who refuse food because of the way it smells or tastes, because of its texture or the way that it looks, have a strong probability of having sensory issues. It is not so much that autism itself predicts avoidant eating but that the attention to the sensory properties of food, and the learned safety component that follows, determines the need to keep to a limited range of foods that are acceptable in terms of their sensory components.

Anxiety, neophobia and sensory sensitivity

As we said in the last chapter, there is a link between sensory hypersensitivity, anxiety and neophobia, as we might expect. The more hypersensitive you are (to smell, to taste, to touch, to visual stimuli), the more you attend to the details in the world around you. Is there anything that is going to smell unpleasant, to feel wrong or look different? If you are always worried about changes in your world, then you become perpetually hypervigilant, watching out for anything different, anything that might pose a threat. This perpetual hypervigilance doesn't help with appetite or with eating. The more anxious we are, the more likely we are to lose our appetite. The more anxious we are, the less likely we are to want to try a new experience. This is true of children. Sensory hypersensitivity in infancy leads to anxiety about the input from the world around them. Children who are reactive to taste, smell and touch become frightened of food, and frightened of eating. So sensory-sensitive children are more worried about trying new foods, and this becomes a real fear response.

Most parents can think of one thing that they are really frightened of: spiders, cows, going over bridges! It is useful to think about your fears. Usually, they are not very rational, and this will help you to understand how a child or adult who is frightened of food feels around mealtimes. If you don't like spiders, would you feel happy sitting in a room with a table covered in creepy crawlies? Would you be happy if someone tried to force you to sit down at the table and play with the spiders? Probably not. This is how an avoidant child feels. The difference is that children have to do as they are told; adults can spend the rest of their lives avoiding spiders and cows and bridges!

Unfortunately, extreme anxiety can also make it difficult to swallow. If a child is very anxious and starts to worry about whether they can swallow the food in their mouth, then it becomes almost impossible to trigger the voluntary part of the swallowing process. Perhaps they have been trying to chew the food for some time. This can lead to a gagging, choking or vomiting response to clear the unprocessed food from the back of the mouth.

Summary

- We have seven senses, the most important of which in terms of food acceptance are taste, smell and touch.

- An eighth sense has been suggested– that of interoception. This is our awareness of internal states such as hunger and pain.

- We differ in how we react to sensory input. Some will be overreactive (hypersensitive), some will be under-reactive (hyposensitive), but it is possible to be overreactive in some domains and under-reactive in others.

- Sensory hypersensitivity is an overreaction to sensory input from the environment.

- Sensitivity to taste and touch can stop a baby from easily accepting new foods when tastes and textures are first introduced.

- Small irrelevant visual details are attended to by those who are sensory-hypersensitive, and this can affect food choices and increase the neophobic response (fear of new foods).

- Older children and adults find certain food textures more difficult to accept if they are sensory-hypersensitive.

- There is a link between sensory sensitivity, neophobia and anxiety.

- Those on the autistic spectrum are more likely to have problems either with hypersensitivity or hyposensitivity to stimuli.

. . .

Tips for parents and carers

If your child has problems with food acceptance, then look carefully to see whether or not they have sensory issues.

Do they:

- dislike being messy, or getting their clothes messy
- prefer clothes of a certain texture
- dislike having their teeth cleaned, their hair washed, their nails cut
- react strongly to food smells, or other smells in the environment
- react to loud noises
- find noisy places uncomfortable
- seem not to experience pain
- seem not to be aware of danger?

. . .

These are just some of the things that you might want to look for. If some of these do seem to be a problem, then, just by being aware that these are real issues for your child, you can begin to help. We give more information on this in Part 2 of the book.

Chapter 4

The Disgust Response
and the Development
of Avoidant Eating

Where have we got to?

The acceptance of food and the willingness to try new foods is largely determined by how a baby or child reacts to sensory information coming in from the environment – that is, how sensory-sensitive they are. Those who are sensory-hypersensitive do not filter out irrelevant stimuli; their brain tries to attend to everything around them. This means that they are often unable to see the wider picture, but attend rather to small, 'local' visual details to determine which foods are safe to eat. Sensory-hypersensitive children also react more strongly to taste, smell and touch, all of which makes them more discerning about which foods and food textures they will accept. Sensory-hypersensitive children are not only more likely to be neophobic, but also more anxious. This too prevents a child from feeling able to try new foods and move on from their restricted diet. Unfortunately, the longer we exclude certain foods from our diet and the more we react to their sensory qualities, the more likely we are to feel a disgust response when faced with those foods.

Disgust and refusal to eat

Many of us can think of a food that we were forced to eat as a child. I can remember at primary school being made to stay behind all through midday play in front of a plate of mushy peas which I just couldn't eat. The smell and the texture of the peas were too awful! I would have sat there all afternoon rather than eat them, but I think that I was eventually allowed to go back to class after playtime was over, even though I still hadn't eaten the peas. I can still remember very precise details about the dining hall I was sitting in. I can remember the curtains, the pictures on the wall, the sun coming through the window and the bench that I was sitting on. This means that this experience was so stressful that I was attending to and remembering things that I didn't need to pay attention to. These memories are still etched into my brain, as are the memories of any very stressful experience. I have never since eaten mushy peas, and I am never likely to. I eat peas in all other forms, even raw in their pods, so this experience did not succeed in getting me to like mushy peas, but rather prevented me from ever eating them.

When asked about why they don't eat certain foods, many adults will say that it is because they were forced to eat them as a child. This led to an extreme dislike and quite often a disgust response. But why was it that these children were forced to eat these foods? We don't force other adults to eat food that they don't like! But adults think that children should eat certain foods. These might be foods that should be in their diet, such as green vegetables. Or it might be thought, when food is scarce, that all food should be eaten up and none wasted. This idea – that food mustn't be wasted and plates should be cleared – can still be seen even where there is no food shortage; it would seem that it is better to overeat than to throw food away! So children are forced to eat foods, and adults hope that by doing this the child will eventually get to like the food. But we have seen that usually that doesn't happen. The problem with any food that we find disgusting is that there is no easy way to get to like it, and no easy way to get that food into the diet of those children, or adults, who can't even face having the food on a plate in front of them. The disgust response is deep-rooted, with good survival value in our primitive past. If we haven't eaten it, if it reminds us of something which might be poisonous, if it reminds us of something which in our culture is a taboo food, if it has made us sick in the past, then we learn very quickly to avoid the food completely. It is a protective mechanism and one which is very deeply rooted in the brain.

Distaste and disgust

We learn not to put things into our mouth that might not be food, or which are foods but which are prohibited by our social group. Usually these foods are banned because they are likely to pose a risk of contamination or infection. But we also avoid foods that, early in infancy, have triggered a distaste/disgust response; an inborn rather than a learned response to foods.

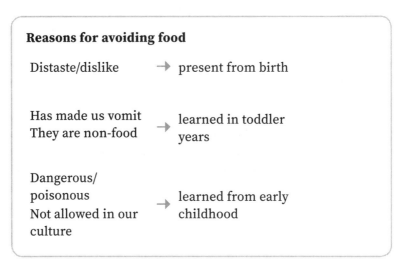

Reasons for avoiding food

Distaste/dislike	→ present from birth
Has made us vomit They are non-food	→ learned in toddler years
Dangerous/ poisonous Not allowed in our culture	→ learned from early childhood

The distaste/disgust response starts in infancy; if the taste or the texture of a food is too extreme, a disgust face and gag can be triggered. This signals to the carer that there might be something wrong with the food given. So a very bitter-tasting food such as broccoli may well trigger quite an extreme response, especially in a sensory-sensitive baby. At a slightly older age, the distaste/disgust response to the visual properties of new foods starts as soon as the toddler can see differences between known 'safe' foods and foods that look different or new.

Toddlers also learn to work out which things that they put in their mouth are foods and which are non-foods! Babies will explore the world with their mouth, but will usually learn by the second year that a wooden toy is not a good source of nutrition, and will learn the rules about substances that pose a danger.

Children with restricted eating patterns, especially where there is developmental delay, might still chew on inappropriate substances while refusing foods. One young boy would chew on wooden toys but refuse all solid foods; when his mother spread jam on one of the toys that he liked to chew, he refused to put it in his mouth again. Somehow that distinction between foods and inappropriate substances is not made and some children will eat non-foods but not foods (pica).

Learned disgust to certain substances and possible foods develops as the toddler gets older and cultural rules are passed on. A baby might eat a worm before the age of 20 months or so but will usually refuse to eat a worm at five years. Toddlers under the age of two years will often put things in their mouth that adults find disgusting (e.g. cat food, the contents of their nappy!), but these are substances that the adults have learned to avoid, and the toddler hasn't yet learned the rules. Some substances, such as faeces and rotting flesh, are universally found to be disgusting and are avoided in most cultures. This disgust response has clear survival benefits and prevents a child from eating something that would be a source of infection. Some rules are culturally specific, and are also learned in childhood. In the UK we tend not to eat insects and most would find them disgusting; in other cultures insects are routinely eaten.

Children also learn which substances are dangerous as they get older. A toddler might drink bleach if it looks like lemonade; an older child will know that the bottle shows that this is not something that can be drunk.

The disgust response can be equally strong where the rule is one specific to a culture. In the bakers, a man returned with a filled roll that he had just bought. He was very upset because he had bitten into it and it contained meat; he was, by religion, vegetarian and had been sold the roll by mistake. He said that he felt contaminated, he felt disgusted, he wanted to clean his mouth out; he felt sick. This is a good example of how strong cultural rules of disgust can be.

Contamination

The distaste/disgust response occurs quite early in life and appears much earlier than other disgust responses such as:

- the disgust response that we feel because of our knowledge of contamination by germs

- our rejection of something that looks like something inedible (raisins looking like rabbit droppings!)

- our rejection of food because of cultural rules.

In toddlers as young as 20 months, when we gave them a liked food that had been touched on the plate by a food that their mother said they didn't like, the toddlers would refuse to eat the liked food even though the disliked food had been taken away out of sight.

And there are differences between children, and between adults, in the strength of their disgust responses, and in the strength of disgust contamination. Some adults will happily eat food that has dropped on the floor or been licked by the dog, whereas others would reject the food straight away. These differences are probably linked to sensory issues and to obsessive-compulsive traits.

Emily had just changed schools (she was 11). She had always had some slight problems with eating but had a reasonable, if slightly limited, diet that she could keep to. She had some contamination fears, though, and liked to keep clean and germ-free. At her new school she stopped eating at lunch time and tried to avoid the meal when she could; she was getting more anxious and losing some weight. Health professionals thought that she might be developing anorexia nervosa. When we talked about what happened at her new school, I found that she had to sit and eat the same meal as the other girls, but, more importantly, at the end of the meal the girls had to take it in turns to clear the plates of all the other girls on the table. She had to touch and smell plates that had had food on them that she couldn't eat and found disgusting. This was enough to stop Emily from eating.

Although there are differences between adults and between children in their response to contamination, what is usually true of all adults and children is that they can all think of at least one food that disgusts them and that would act as a contaminant. The foods that adults usually report as being disgusting to them are those foods with difficult textures or strong smells.

Texture:

- slimy (bananas, mushrooms)

- slimy and chewy (shellfish, liver)

- multiple textures and mixed foods (tomatoes, rice pudding)

Smell:

- strong smell (ripe bananas, eggs).

Each of these attributes might either have strong sensory components or signal the possibility of contamination by bacteria.

Imagine your disgust food; think about it. Now imagine that I have hidden your disgust food (banana, shellfish, liver, slugs?) inside a sandwich which usually has a filling in that you like. You bite into it, and your mouth fills with the taste and texture of the disgust food. Will you ever accept a sandwich from me again? Is this likely to make you eat your disgust food?

A slug sandwich!

Each disgust food acts as a contaminant for other foods. If a disgust food touches another on the plate, then none of the foods can be eaten. Some children will carefully move disgust foods away from foods that they will eat; others will be unable to eat anything on the plate once the disgust food has been placed on it. This means that it is not a sensible idea to put a new food on a child's plate next to their preferred food, especially if they are a fussy eater; the new food can act as a contaminant for the whole meal.

There is a difference, though, in the degree of disgust that a food can generate, and this depends on the properties of the food. One mother told me that she felt disgust towards both sweetcorn and shellfish, but if sweetcorn was on her plate next to liked foods, she could just move it away. However, if there was shellfish on the plate, she would have to refuse the whole plate of food. Slimy foods are always those that are most likely to act as contaminants.

One food can contaminate another

Hidden foods

We have discussed in previous chapters something that adults often do to get children to eat disliked foods. They try to hide a refused food in something that is usually eaten – for example, chopping vegetables small and adding them into another meal. Parents will often say that they have tried this with their child and it worked, but these are parents who don't have an avoidant or sensory-sensitive child. Disgust responses are more extreme in the sensory-hypersensitive child. Hiding a food that a child finds disgusting in a liked meal can lead to an extreme refusal response in the child.

Mixed foods are always more difficult for avoidant children to accept, and they are the foods most likely to be rejected in the neophobic stage. This is because it is difficult to identify the individual components of the food, the mixed texture is difficult to process and a 'mixed' dish is likely to look different each time it is prepared. But if a child has been fed a specific recipe from infancy (such as shepherd's pie), then they can quite happily get to learn to like the taste and texture combinations.

What becomes difficult is when the adult decides that mushrooms cut very small can be hidden in the dish and the child won't notice. But if the child is sensory-sensitive, they will notice, and either reject the whole dish or spend the mealtime picking out very small pieces of mushroom. We have to think: is it worth losing a meal that is readily accepted just to get those mushrooms in? Sometimes adding things to food that is accepted can lose one of the staple foods in the diet; it might work, but usually it doesn't, so is it worth the risk?

Some parents can hide food, insist that their child eat their vegetables and try all sorts of strategies that seem to work for them. They are lucky: they have children who don't have a fear of food. What works for them won't necessarily work for other children. What works and what doesn't work depends upon the child. It is always important to trust the child rather than listen to advice from other parents who don't have a child similar to yours.

Safe to eat?

So, for some toddlers moving into the neophobic stage, the disgust response develops quite markedly and can become very strong. And we need to remember that the disgust response in all of its stages is protective. In the early stages the disgust response stops us from eating any substance or any food that looks or smells as if it is likely to cause us harm. So the look and smell of the food contributes to our assessment of whether or not it is safe to eat. Many parents will report that their avoidant child started to refuse foods in the neophobic stage and that this continued with an ever-decreasing range of foods accepted. These children are worried about the 'safety' of the food that they are eating. Will it taste the same? Will it feel the same in my mouth? Is this the food that I know and am happy with?

Any attempts to get a child to eat a food that they don't feel is 'safe' will:

- increase their anxiety levels

- make them more hypervigilant

- decrease their appetite.

Even if you get the food into their mouth, they are unlikely to swallow it.

As the food is repeatedly rejected or avoided, especially if there is any pressure to eat the food, so the disgust response develops and strengthens, and the disgust response is one which the brain likes to hang on to! The higher the anxiety levels, the more the disgust response will increase. A mild disgust response can become a fixed response if the child is made to feel anxious around the food or is made to eat the food. On the other hand, a mild disgust response can be modified downwards if the child isn't made to feel anxious, if others are eating the food and if eating the food is under the child's control.

A health professional told me that her father, who came from a coastal region in East Asia, was exposed early and often to 'slimy' shellfish and fish during his early childhood. At family meals, even before he experienced the taste of the foods, he was exposed to the sight and smell of them. He happily ate all of these culturally appropriate foods – but could not stand cheese! This is because cheese would not have been a food that was culturally available and so hadn't been introduced to his diet at an early age. And cheese is a difficult food to accept because of the smell and texture; even around 10 per cent of the French cannot eat it!

Disgust response as a result of not eating a food!

The longer that you don't eat a food, the more difficult it becomes to get it into your mouth. Why this is – that some foods if not eaten will become disgusting, even if you have never tasted them – is not clearly understood. We know that foods of certain textures, slimy rather than dry and crunchy, are more likely to be found disgusting – for good reason. We know that if you feel anxious when you are near a food, and if someone has pressured you to eat it, then you are more likely to feel disgust. We also know that we can have some idea of what a food might taste like, or even the feel of the food in the mouth, just by looking at the food. And those who are more anxious in general are more likely to have a higher disgust response.

So these things added up will ensure that an avoidant child

- with a limited dietary range

- who is sensory-sensitive

- who might often be coaxed to eat refused foods

is likely to have a range of foods that evoke the disgust response, even though those foods have never been tried.

But sometimes something has been tried, and even though it was so long ago it still evokes the disgust response by association.

Vegetarian meat pies are made to look and smell like meat. Helen and I are both vegetarian, but neither Helen nor I can put meat substitutes in our mouth. They provoke a disgust response, and yet we had different reasons for giving up on meat. I disliked the texture of meat as a young child and refused to eat it when I gained control over my diet. Helen loved meat, but gave it up in because she had ethical objections to eating it. When we were younger, the pre-prepared meat-substitute foods weren't around, so neither of us got used to them. Now we cannot eat meat substitutes, after many years of not eating meat, just because we have ethical or sensory reasons for the rejection of meat-based products. It should be that Helen, whose rejection was not for reasons of sensory/distaste, should be able to eat something that she knows not to be meat, but this is not the case.

Disgust at others eating

The disgust response doesn't stop at not eating a specific food when it is put in front of you; it can generalise to the environment and what others around you are doing. The smell of food and the effect that this can have on children's food acceptance hasn't been well researched, but we know from what children say that it can be important. Adults who cannot eat bananas will often say that the smell disgusts them before they can even touch the fruit. The smell of disgust foods puts us off even going near them. Again, this would have been beneficial to early humans, and this is a response often seen in other mammals – smell warns us to stay away. Avoidant children can find the smell of the food that their family is eating disgusting; the food is disgusting to them and so is the smell. These children find it difficult to sit at meal tables with their family and will only eat in another room.

Similarly, the sound of others eating can trigger a disgust response in the sensory-hypersensitive child (and adult). The sound of chewing on noisy foods such as apples or crisps is often found disgusting, as is the sight of someone eating with less than polite table manners. So eating with an open mouth, talking while eating, licking fingers or cutlery can all be off-putting to the sensory-sensitive fussy eater. And the more anxious or stressed you are, the more you respond to the sound, smell and sight of others eating.

Michael, aged 8, had problems eating his packed lunch in the dining hall. He had to sit with the other children who were eating their packed lunches, so the smell and sight of their food that he found disgusting didn't help. Unfortunately, the other boys in his class knew that Michael had some problems with food, and one particular boy used to like to wind him up by waving his food under Michael's nose. One day this escalated: the other boy sat close to Michael and started to eat noisily with his mouth open. Michael hit the other boy and was sent home. I think the wrong child was punished!

This often means that avoidant children often cannot eat in the school dining hall and will eat better if allowed to eat away from the other children. Parents have reported that their school insists that their child sits in the dining hall with their packed lunch, and that when this happens the packed lunch always comes back home uneaten.

Moving on

Not all foods that are excluded from the diet will give rise to a strong disgust response. When the child is old enough to start trying new foods themselves, some foods will be easier to get into the mouth than others. Those foods that won't disgust are often those that are most similar in smell, taste, texture and appearance to foods that are already eaten. This is why, when moving on, it is important to ask the child what they think they would like to try. They will usually choose those foods that they are wary of but which don't disgust. Often they will just choose another version of a biscuit already accepted! But it is important not to start the intervention process too early using foods which might disgust. This can be very de-motivating for the child.

> Peter, at 15, was moving on with introducing new foods into his diet and was gaining confidence in trying different things. He could eat bread and tomato and cheese, so he thought he could have a salad sandwich. When he was out with some friends, he thought he would try one, but biting into it brought on a very strong disgust response to some cucumber. He described it as slimy and had to spit it all out. Peter was very upset by this and thought that he had made a move backwards rather than forwards. Thinking about it, however, he decided that he could probably live without cucumber in his life. Most of us have one or two foods that we can't eat, and cucumber was going to be one of his.

Summary

- There are five reasons for food aversion: distaste/disgust, learned disgust, culturally defined disgust, learned consequences of eating and that the substance is not a food.
- Disgust responses to extreme taste and textures can be seen from infancy.
- Some foods – those that are slimy and smelly – are more likely to trigger a disgust response than are others.
- Learned 'cognitive' disgust develops in mid-childhood.
- Some children will not learn to avoid non-foods, but will still find foods disgusting.
- Avoidant children tend to show higher disgust sensitivity.
- The disgust response is increased by anxiety.
- Disgust foods contaminate other foods.
- There is an individual hierarchy of disgust; some foods are more disgusting than others.
- Foods that have never been eaten can also trigger a disgust response.

. . .

Tips for parents and carers

- Never force, persuade or coerce your child into eating a food that they cannot put into the mouth.
- If your child shows some reluctance to eat a food, stay very calm! Eat it yourself instead.
- The more you increase stress and anxiety around food and mealtimes, the more extreme the disgust response will be.
- Disgust foods act as contaminants to liked foods. Never put them on the plate together.
- Extreme disgust responses can cause gagging, retching and vomiting. Although these behaviours

should always be checked by a health professional, they could just be a response to food.

- Some foods are so disgusting that the child, or adult, cannot even be near them or in the same room. This is also true of other people eating.

. . .

Chapter 5

Appetite and Appetite Regulation

Where have we got to?

We learn to accept different foods by watching others around us eat them. Infants are exposed to the taste, smell and sight of foods that are available and safe to eat. Some tastes are more likely to be avoided – a bitter taste is one of these – and there are inborn differences in taste sensitivity. Some textures, such as those that are slimy, are also more likely to be avoided. There are good survival reasons for the avoidance of these tastes and textures. There are also differences in how sensory-sensitive children are – that is, how much they respond to the tastes, smells, textures and the sight of food. Sensory hypersensitivity affects both the acceptance of tastes and textures in infancy and the extent of the neophobic response (fear of new foods) at around 20 months. The disgust response to food can also be seen from infancy through to childhood and adulthood, but there is more than one reason for this response to develop. It is either triggered by the sensory properties of the food, by learned consequences or by learned cultural rules. However, all of this learning about which foods to accept or reject is not the same as knowing how *much* food to eat.

How much do we need?

As adults, we eat the amount of food that we need to provide our bodies with the energy necessary for us to breathe, to move, to live. Children also need to take in enough food to keep themselves and their bodies going, as well as eating enough calories to allow them to grow to their full potential. But the amount of food needed is different for every child; this is true even for children of the same age, because they have different growth and energy needs. Some children are shorter than others and so need less food.

The only way that you can really know if your child is growing as they should be, and eating enough for them, is to check their growth on their growth chart. Look at the centile chart that is in the parent-held records or in their medical records. Your child should be following along the same centile lines from early in the first year though to later childhood. Look first at their height. Is it tracking along a centile line? Then look at their weight: it should be following roughly the same line; it may be a bit below or a bit above, but there should be no more than two centile lines' difference. If your child is growing along their centile lines as they should be, then they are eating enough for them. If the weight line is well underneath the height line, then your child is eating too little; if it is well above the height line, then they are eating too much.

Some children, of course, are born to be shorter and smaller than others; this is usually genetically determined and smaller parents are likely to have smaller children. Looking at a centile chart, the small children will follow their centile line just like the taller children. Centile lines just describe the population that they are measuring. There will be some short children and some very tall children. If your child's height and weight are following the bottom centiles and always have done, then giving extra food will not make them grow taller – it will just make them fatter!

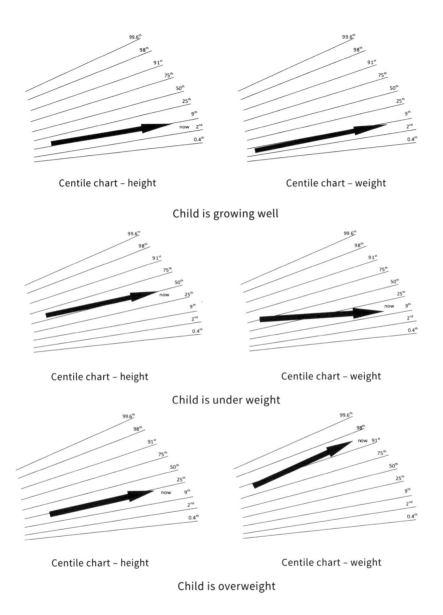

Centile chart – height   Centile chart – weight

Child is growing well

Centile chart – height   Centile chart – weight

Child is under weight

Centile chart – height   Centile chart – weight

Child is overweight

How much your child needs to eat is then determined by their size and their rate of growth. Small children need less food than tall children, just as tall men need more food than small women.

Your child's metabolic rate – that is, how fast the body is burning up calories – also helps to determine how many calories they need to live and grow. Every child's metabolic rate is different. Fidgety, energetic children need more food than placid children, just because they burn up more calories.

So some children will need to eat less than others, and some will need to eat more than others. We don't always need to worry if a child is smaller and eats less than their friends. If they are increasing in height and weight at a steady rate, then they are eating the right amount.

Regulation and compensation

So, how do we know how much to eat? Whether or not the stomach is full is only really a short-term regulator of appetite and how hungry we feel. Deciding whether or not to eat and how much to eat is a complex process involving both the gut and the brain.

We should really only eat the calories we need for our day-to-day activities and cell renewal and then stop eating, but we aren't really designed to do this. As hunter-gatherers, our ancestors might have had days when there was a glut of food – after a big kill perhaps – and days when there was little food available. So when food is available constantly, we might just eat to our needs, but if there are days when food is not available, then we will compensate. This means that on some days we will eat large amounts to try to take in the calories that we have missed when food was not available. These two processes are called regulation and compensation. We should regulate our intake according to our needs on a daily basis, but if food is not available, then we will compensate at a later time by eating a much larger amount.

What we cannot do is regulate the balance of our diet. If we are hungry or have missed a meal, then we will mostly just eat those foods that we have learned to like or are happy eating, but just in larger amounts! If we are travelling, and there is no food anywhere that we like, then when we do finally come to a café where we can get something that we like, we will usually eat as much as we can! We are making up for the period of starvation. This is an important point to remember when thinking about how avoidant children might eat. They will often eat nothing if the food that they like is not available, but eat all that they can when their 'safe' food is available.

This kind of eating can also be seen in adults who try to restrict their eating because they have concerns about their body shape (bulimia nervosa, binge eating disorder). After a while they cannot maintain the restriction and then 'binge eat' all that they can. This is a similar mechanism to the overeating sometimes seen in avoidant children. However, the restricted intake that precedes the 'binge eating' in avoidant children has nothing to do with concerns about body image, nor do children feel ashamed about how much they eat. They just know that they are hungry.

Jonnie, aged 13, was not allowed to take any foods to school that were 'safe' for him. He wasn't allowed to take packed lunches and had to eat in the school canteen. Occasionally, something would be served that he could eat, but often nothing was there that he liked. His mother was worried that he was binge eating when he came home from school. He would eat almost half a loaf of bread as soon as he walked through the door. But in fact he was just showing compensatory eating, making up for calories he should have eaten during the day. His weight was good for his height and he was growing well; he was not overeating.

Responding to cues to eat

As adults, every day we eat what we normally eat and when we normally eat it, and children learn to do this too from early infancy. We usually have the same food at the same time of day with the same portion size. Having said this, we also know that there are differences between children and adults in how aware they are of internal cues to appetite and how responsive they are to food cues. Some children do not easily respond to cues of fullness (satiety) and will continue to want to eat even though they have just had a big meal. Between meals, these children will be looking out for food; they might keep asking for biscuits or sweets. They will also eat more than they need at any one mealtime; they just keep asking for more. Other children and adults are the opposite of this; they are not really tuned in to whether or not they are hungry. It is very easy to put them off eating, by giving food that they don't like, or don't feel like, eating. There are also differences in how 'responsive' children and adults are to food cues; if food is around and available, then some children just feel the need to eat it, whether they feel hungry or not. Others will just ignore the food and not have to eat it just because it is available.

Peter will eat an entire packet of biscuits if they are left where he can get to them. He says, after he has eaten them all, that he feels quite uncomfortable, but this doesn't stop him from doing it again. Maddy would only eat two biscuits even if the whole packet was there; she wouldn't want to eat any more and can leave the opened packet without finishing them all. Peter's wife has to hide the biscuits underneath the vegetables!

Learning to be hungry

Leaving a child for a long time between meals does not, however, make them eat food they don't like. And giving more frequent meals and snacks throughout the day is the best way to maximise the amount of food eaten and to keep meals stress-free.

We learn to be hungry at the times that we would normally eat, or are normally fed. If we have breakfast at 7am, we are hungry for breakfast at 7am. If we don't usually eat until coffee-break time, then that is when we start to get hungry for a little something. A child with a poor appetite or feeding difficulties will put on more weight if they are fed frequently; short, frequent mealtimes are the better option. This is because long mealtimes can be stressful for the child, and after around 20 minutes a child will have eaten most of what they are going to eat at that meal. The more small meals they are given, the more a child learns to be hungry at different times during the day and will increase their intake. Of course, if a parent is dealing with a child who is overweight, then they need to remember that frequent snacks will lead to weight gain!

Similarly, we learn the calorie load of the foods that we have in our diet. So, in order to take the calories we need across the day, the brain and body need to know that a specific meal – perhaps a sandwich – has certain number of calories (perhaps 350kcals). We learn to eat the foods that we know, with the calorie load that we are used to, across the day as part of our routine meals and snacks; we will then usually take in the calorie load that we need for that day.

Think about a time when you have been rushed and missed your usual meal. Quite often you will stop at a shop or a garage and pick up a snack. A high-fat and high-sugar snack probably has the same number of calories as the sandwich you have just missed out on. When your body needs to compensate, you reach for the high-calorie snack – it is a quick and easy way to get energy in. This is why it is so difficult to go on a diet; your body keeps telling you to compensate for all of the calories you have taken out of your daily intake, usually with a quick snack!

The calorie load of each food and each meal needs to be learned, and babies can do this from birth, so that they can regulate their intake. Remember, it is the baby who determines how much breast milk is taken at each feed, not the mother. Young infants and children tend to be better at this regulation; they are more likely than adults and older children to only take what they need. Adults and older children are more influenced by social cues to overeat.

Balancing the diet

Although children, as well as adults, are usually hungry for the calories that they need throughout the day, there is no real mechanism that means that they will want to eat the balance of foods that they need to make up a 'healthy' diet.

We might think that we crave the foods we need, but this craving is usually confined to foods and drinks that can quickly alter our mood or blood sugar levels, such as sweet foods or caffeine-containing drinks. The brain isn't designed to send us off in search of fruit because we haven't had enough vitamin C that day. The brain and body rely on the fact that, as foragers and omnivores, we will eventually meet all of our dietary requirements.

What does happen, though, is that if we eat too much of one food, day after day, we will lose our appetite for it. This is one way in which the brain can make us go out and forage for something else at the supermarket if we have been eating too many pizzas. Quite often we don't notice that this is happening; we have so many foods in our diet that the sudden feeling that we cannot face another avocado doesn't really bother us. However, for children who have a very restricted diet this can be worrying for parents. If a child eats only 6 foods, then to lose one of them can feel like a major crisis. Surprisingly, though, when one food goes, another will often come in from somewhere else.

Because we know that the more frequently a food is eaten, the more likely it is to be dropped, it is always a good idea to vary the foods that your child will eat across the days. Where this is possible, it will help to keep all of those foods eaten by the child in their diet.

New foods might come into the diet because the child has seen the food advertised on television, or because a teacher offered the food at a school fete, or because the child liked the smell of the food at a Christmas market. The food that gets introduced is seemingly always the child's choice and not the parent's choice. Oddly, though, although I have known many children who will eat crisps as part of their restricted diet, I have never known them to be dropped from the diet because they have eaten them too often!

Social influences

Although we eat when our bodies tell us we are hungry, we also eat for other reasons. Children and adults will usually eat when others are eating, even if they are not particularly hungry. In our past this would have led us to eat when food was available for our social group. So we often eat more at social mealtimes. We eat foods when we see others eat them, even though we often wouldn't usually eat at that time.

We also tend to eat larger portions than we need if others serve out our food for us, and if they eat large portions themselves. Many adults think that you should finish all that is on your plate, so if you are given too much, you eat too much! Children do this too: if adults serve out larger portions to a child than they would normally eat, then the child will eat more. This is most likely to be true, however, for those children who are responsive to foods cues, rather than to fussy children who don't respond well to hunger cues. Very often an avoidant child will be reported as being very slow to eat their meal. This is either because they have been given too large a portion or because they don't really like the food that they have been given.

When we are running training days for health professionals, we often see participants eating cakes and biscuits that are provided as they arrive for the day, at around 9am. Everyone stands around with tea and a pastry. If we ask if they would normally have a cake at that time of day, usually everyone says 'No'. They are eating the food because it is there and because everyone else is eating it!

Children with restricted intakes tend not to respond to social cues to overeat. They don't imitate other people's eating habits and tend not to eat more than they need. They can eat a lot of their accepted food at just one mealtime, especially if their accepted foods have been withheld during the day. They are just trying to get all of their calories in at one go.

What will stop a child from eating?

Supplementary feeding

If a child is taking most of their calories from another source, then they will not be hungry for food.

Some infants might still be totally or mainly reliant on breast or bottle feeds into their second year. This might be because they have had problems with the acceptance of foods, or because they have had medical procedures or conditions that prevented the introduction of solid foods at an appropriate time. If this is so, then all of their calorie and energy needs will be met by the milk diet, and they will not be hungry enough to want to try new foods.

Similarly, if a child is tube-fed and is now following along the expected growth centiles (their weight is on the same centile line as their height, or even above the height line), then the child will not feel hungry for any additional food. Even if the tube feed is given overnight, the brain still counts those calories, and appetite will be reduced.

Unfortunately, avoidant children:

- because they are so reluctant to try new foods, and

- because they have so many problems with the acceptance of the taste and textures of new foods,

are often very happy to stay on their tube feeds, and see no reason to move on to eating food.

Sometimes as well, because of poor growth or poor diet, children are prescribed high-calorie dietary supplements, usually drinks or puddings. Although these will work in the short term to help with weight gain, after a few weeks they usually serve to reduce the normal food intake, so that calorie intake is back to where it was at the beginning of the regime.

Caroline was 14 months old. She had eaten well in early infancy and had been introduced to the different food textures and tastes at the appropriate times. Unfortunately, at around nine months she needed to have a medical procedure which meant that she had to be totally tube-fed for a few months. However, when she was well, her parents couldn't get her back to eating again; even if she put food in her mouth, she would just store it there and not swallow it. When we looked at her weight and height in clinic, we could see what the problem was. Caroline was overweight for her height; she had no appetite for food. Her parents gradually reduced the amount fed to her through her tube, and soon she was accepting food and quickly weaned off the tube. Caroline was not sensory-sensitive or food-avoidant so the process was easy.

Illness

Short-term illnesses might well stop a child from eating, and if a child only eats very few foods, this can be very worrying. Most of us lose our appetite when we are unwell, especially if we are running a temperature, and in the short term we will lose some weight. But once a child is well again, their appetite will return and the weight will be regained; the child will show compensatory eating. This is true of children who are avoidant eaters as well as those children who eat well. Some children also get very worried when they vomit as part of their illness. Children who are very food-avoidant get especially worried about vomiting and will often be reluctant to eat foods that might make them vomit again.

Constipation

One of the problems that is often reported with children with a limited-range diet is that of constipation; limited-range diets are usually poor in terms of dietary fibre because children are not happy eating fruits and vegetables. Constipation affects a child's entire digestive system. It slows down the rate at which food moves from the stomach into the gut. If food is moving slowly through the gut, then signals are sent to the brain which will reduce appetite and the desire to eat. Children with constipation will not want to eat and their intake will be poor until they have a bowel movement, so it is very important that a child has regular bowel movements. Constipation should always be treated in order to regulate a child's intake and keep their growth on track. It should never be assumed that parents can improve their child's diet sufficiently to resolve the constipation if their child is an avoidant eater.

Parents in clinic would often report that their avoidant child would have some very good days when they would eat very well, some very, very poor days when they would eat hardly anything at all, and some days in between, when they would eat bits and pieces. We usually found that good and bad days mapped on to when the child had had a bowel movement. When they had just had a bowel movement, they would eat very well, over the next few days they would eat reasonably well, and then, if they hadn't had a bowel movement, they would stop eating! With medication to give a regular pattern to bowel movements, intake became more predictable across the week.

Iron-deficient anaemia

If the child has a diet which is very low in foods containing iron, then they are likely to become anaemic – iron-deficient anaemia. Children who are anaemic become very noticeably tired and look very pale. Unfortunately, the anaemia and the tiredness can decrease their appetite, and they will not feel like eating. If there are few iron-rich foods in the child's diet and they have a poor appetite, then it is important for parents to see a health professional to check to see if their child is anaemic. If anaemia is left untreated, then appetite and food intake will continue to decrease, and the child will lose weight. If the child is anaemic, they can be prescribed iron supplement tablets, or parents can be given dietary advice on how to include more foods in the diet which are high in iron. An increase in dietary iron will improve appetite. Surprisingly, good chocolate is a source of dietary iron, although not the best one, and as many children with a restricted diet will eat chocolate, iron-deficient anaemia is not as prevalent amongst these children as it might be.

Stress

Children, like adults, cope with stress and pressure in different ways. Sometimes stress makes us eat more, quite quickly, to increase our blood sugar levels; sometimes we eat less to prepare for the 'fight or flight' response. Mostly, however, if a child is made to feel pressured or anxious about food or eating, they will start to lose their appetite. They may then not feel like eating and begin to avoid food. Quite often these children will eat more at snack times than at mealtimes. This is because they are not being pressured to eat at snack times and stress levels are lower, whereas at mealtimes an anxious parent might be trying to persuade them to eat more. Mealtimes should always be kept as calm as possible and children should never be forced to eat.

A study carried out after the Second World War looked at children in care homes in Germany. Widdowson, who carried out the research, was interested in dietary intake and growth, and so to study this she changed the diet that was given to the children in different care homes. Surprisingly, though, where she had increased the energy intake for one group to compare with the other, she found that the children's weight did not increase. The dietitian who had been measuring growth and intake pointed out that a very stern matron had transferred to the children's home just as the food intake was increased. She made a point of scolding and disciplining the children at mealtimes, so although they ate the extra food, they did not put on extra weight (Widdowson 1951). Stress at mealtimes would seem to alter the way in which nutrients are metabolised – that is, how much food is used up quickly and how much is stored by the body.

Stress in general can also affect appetite. If a child is feeling unhappy about things that are happening, at home, at school or with friends, it may affect their eating. Some children may comfort eat, but usually avoidant children will not feel like eating at all. Here, eating is not really the problem and, rather than focus on mealtimes, parents need to work out what else is worrying the child.

It could be that:

- a routine has changed at school

- they are being bullied at school

- they cannot cope with school lunch times because of the other children and what they are eating.

When these problems have been dealt with, then their eating should return to normal.

In clinic we often found that children would show a return of their restricted diet in September, even if they had improved during the summer holiday. They would go back to eating only very few safe foods. This was because they had to face a new term at school with a new teacher, a new classroom, a new routine. Parents quickly learned to accept the regression to 'just the few foods', knowing that when their child was settled in at school, their dietary range would increase again.

Summary

- Babies and children can regulate their intake to match their growth and energy needs.

- Growth and energy needs differ from child to child; short children need less food than tall children of the same age.

- The only way to check on a child's growth is to plot their height and weight on a centile chart.

- If meals are missed, then we compensate by eating more later in that day, or later in the week.

- This compensatory eating can look like binge eating in an avoidant child.

- Older children and adults might eat more than they need if they are prompted to eat more, if they are given larger portion sizes than they need or if others around them are eating too much.

- Some children and adults are more6 responsive to food cues and will eat when they don't really need to; other children and adults are not aware of their hunger signals and don't eat when they should.

- We can only regulate the amount of food that we eat, not the type of foods that we eat; so we do not eat specific foods to maintain dietary balance.

- However, if we eat too much of one food, we will lose our appetite for that food.

- If babies and children are bottle-fed, tube-fed or given dietary supplements, and their weight is appropriate for their height, then they will have no appetite for food.

- Stress, illness, anaemia and constipation can all reduce appetite for food.

. . .

Tips for parents and carers

- Don't worry if your child seems to be eating less than other children of the same age. Check their weight against their height – they are probably growing as they should do.

- Don't prompt children to finish up what is on their plate; let them decide how much they need to eat.

- Allow avoidant children their safe foods rather than withholding them to make them eat new foods. Good growth is more important in childhood than a varied diet.

- Give avoidant children small frequent meals throughout the day.
- If your child is pale and lethargic, do check with a health professional to ensure that they are not anaemic, and ask for help if your child is constipated.
- Any milk feeds or supplementary feeds that your baby or child is having will contribute to their calorie load; they might then not be hungry for food, so ask a health professional for help in reducing these feeds.

. . .

Chapter 6

What Is Avoidant and Restrictive Food Intake Disorder?

Where have we got to?

Children learn to like the foods that they are given in infancy. These are foods that would be appropriate to their cultural group and therefore easily available. Babies get used to the tastes, the smell, the feel of the foods and the way that that these foods look. When they reach the neophobic stage at around the age of 20 months, however, children will start to refuse foods that look different from foods that they are used to. These foods will be refused on sight. Gradually, most children develop out of this neophobic stage and begin to start to try new and different foods by about five years of age. They are more likely to try the new foods if they see others eat them, and if they get to touch and interact with the foods.

However, this whole process is more difficult for those children who are sensory-hypersensitive – that is, those children who respond more to incoming sensory stimuli. These children are more sensitive to the taste, the smell, the feel and the look of the foods that they are given. They are more likely to refuse foods both in infancy and during the neophobic stage. Their dietary intake can be very restricted and their response to food can be fearful. They only eat foods that they feel are 'safe' for them. They show higher levels of disgust towards unknown foods, and greater contamination fears. Unknown foods can make them gag and vomit. We would call these children 'avoidant eaters', rather than just a little 'fussy'. However, if avoidant eaters are allowed to eat their 'safe' foods, they will grow as expected.

Avoidant children with restricted diets

Many professionals working with children who refuse to eat have thought for many years that there was a group of children who had real difficulties with food acceptance. The usual intervention strategies that were suggested did not work for these children.

> Parents will often tell of advice given to them that didn't work:
> - 'Leave them; they will eat when they are hungry.'
> - 'Make them sit in front of the food until they eat it.'
> - 'They will eat when they go to nursery school and see the other children eating.'

Parents would seem to have tried all reasonable strategies without success, and often had other children in the family who ate well, but there was something different about the way that these children felt about food. Parents would report how they had gone from health professional to health professional without finding anyone who understood the problem and they would also report that they were often given unhelpful or contradictory advice.

> One health professional suggested to a family with a child with a restricted diet that a meal (spaghetti bolognaise) should be put in front of the child at teatime and should be left there until it was eaten. If it wasn't eaten, it should be put in the fridge and given again the next day, until it was eaten.

This sort of advice was not atypical and was common because the eating behaviour was not recognised for what it was. This eating behaviour is also relatively rare; many health professionals would not have seen a child with this sort of problem with food before. It was often thought that the child was being naughty or stubborn or 'exercising their "no" muscles'. If a child had milder difficulties with food, then forcing them to eat food that they didn't like might well work – it would get eaten. This doesn't mean, however, that the child would choose to eat the food in the future. If I was locked in a cellar for a long period, I might well eat the cat food that I found there; this doesn't mean that I would add cat food to my diet when I next went to the supermarket.

The arrival of ARFID

After much consultation, in 2013, this extreme reaction to food was finally recognised as an eating disorder in the American *Diagnostic and Statistical Manual of Mental Disorders* (DSM-5). It has been described as: Avoidant and Restrictive Food Intake Disorder (ARFID).

The defining characteristics, according to DSM-5, are that the child:

- doesn't seem hungry. There is a lack of interest in eating and the child will go for long periods without food or asking for food

- avoids foods because of their sensory characteristics. The child is sensory-hypersensitive and reacts to the sight, taste, texture and smell of food

- may be concerned about the consequences of eating foods or certain foods. They might be worried about choking or vomiting

- may fail to gain weight, but this is more likely where 'safe' and accepted foods are withheld or not available

- may show nutritional deficits because of the limited range of foods that are accepted

- might need tube-feeding, but this is usually a last resort because it is very difficult to wean an avoidant child from tube feeds once these have started

- has problems with social situations because of their avoidant eating and restricted diet. The child might be very anxious around food and therefore unable to join in with family mealtimes or social activities where food is involved

In addition to this, based on our clinical experience, children who would receive a diagnosis of ARFID would meet the following criteria.

They:

- will only eat very few foods (range 5–10)

- show brand loyalty (the packaging predicts the safety of the food)

- only eat one flavour of an accepted food

- eat certain foods specific to context

- show extreme anxiety if offered new foods or foods that they don't like

- may gag or vomit if offered disliked foods

- are usually boys

- usually show strong cross-modal hypersensitivity

- often receive a diagnosis of autistic spectrum disorder, but not necessarily so.

Describing the child with ARFID

Those children who would be classified as having ARFID have a very restricted diet and have problems accepting new foods. Their diet usually consists of a few foods with very specific textures. The textures are usually dry and easily processed in the mouth. Foods of this texture tend to be carbohydrate, and because of this specific texture requirement, they tend to be brown or beige. In addition, the child might eat soft pureed food with smooth textures, such as first-stage baby food, yoghurt or custard, and sometimes bite-and-melt foods such as chocolate.

The problems that these children have with food acceptance are most likely to have been noticed at the age of the introduction of lumpy-textured solids (seven to ten months); some infants, however, may have had difficulties accepting a range of tastes in earlier infancy. A smaller group of children seem to have accepted first foods quite readily but then started to refuse more and more foods as they progressed through the neophobic stage.

All children would be described as highly neophobic, but this would not be confined to just a fear of new foods; it would also include a fear of any food that looked slightly different from the usual method of presentation.

This adherence to foods that are 'known to be safe' means that children with ARFID show extreme brand loyalty. They can tell the difference between the taste of different breads and can see the difference between brands of the same kind of biscuit. Any food that tastes, smells or looks different from the accepted food will be rejected. The packaging of the food predicts the 'safety' of the food; any changes to packaging will lead to rejection of that food on sight. In some cases a child can tell the difference between known foods and new foods even by the smell, without tasting.

Kelly was totally blind from birth and on the autistic spectrum. She would eat digestive biscuits – one brand only. If she was offered another brand, she would take it in her hand and throw it away without putting it near her mouth. She could smell the difference between the biscuits.

Joseph would eat a blended meat stew but could tell if his mother had added vegetables to it just by the smell, even though it still looked the same. He would reject the stew without tasting it.

Any food that is not the same as an accepted food can trigger a disgust response. Disgust leads to the rejection of foods and increases stress levels at mealtimes, especially if disliked foods are offered. Any attempt to get the child to eat a non-accepted food can lead to an extreme fear response with heightened anxiety. Stress and anxiety around food and at mealtimes leads to hypervigilance and therefore increases attention to differences between known and new foods; the fear response is made worse. Food is rejected on sight, and these children find it difficult to accept food that looks slightly different from known foods. This is because they are concentrating on the specific details of each food or food packaging; it then becomes difficult to see one food as 'the same as' a similar food.

Children with this behaviour do not easily imitate others' eating behaviour. They will not modify their eating behaviour to fit in with the habits and preferences of others, as other children often can. Usually, as children develop out of the neophobic stage, they will start to imitate other children around them. They will want to try foods that they see others eat. Children with a diagnosis of ARFID will rarely copy another's eating behaviour because of their anxiety about the new food – the way it might taste or feel in the mouth. Their disgust response is also so high that they cannot bring themselves to try it.

> We might want to jump off the top diving board as our friends seem able to do. We might even manage to go and stand on the top diving board. But if we have a fear of heights, or if we are just terrified of what might happen when we jump, we will not be able to dive in, even if our best friend is happily jumping in before us.

Children with a diagnosis of ARFID are very likely to have sensory issues in all sensory domains, and this will have an impact on other areas of their life. The smell of food at home mealtimes might cause them to want to eat in another room; they might find it difficult to eat in school dining halls where the smell of cooked meals can be unpleasant for them. They might find it difficult to eat out in a restaurant, but this could also be because of the noise in the room or the number of other people around them. If they are made to sit with the family at mealtimes, their stress and anxiety levels increase. Where anxiety levels increase, attention to detail also increases and food is less likely to be tried or accepted.

Harry was given a diagnosis of ARFID. Harry's father realised that his own problems with food were similar to Harry's, and subsequently he was given a diagnosis of Asperger's syndrome. Harry's father explained how difficult he found it if he had to eat out in a restaurant. It wasn't only the food; he would feel anxious about the whole process and then could not screen out everything that was going on around him. He would eventually be overwhelmed by the noise, by others around him and their conversations; he could never just attend to what his wife was saying.

Sensory sensitivity contributes to the neophobic response, and to the fear of foods. And the fear of being asked to eat foods that are not 'safe' adds to anxiety felt around mealtimes. It is likely that this anxiety follows on from heightened sensory sensitivity to incoming stimuli present in early infancy. It could be, however, that children with ARFID are innately more anxious. Children with ARFID are also likely to show more 'general' neophobia – fear of any new events or objects in their environment. In addition, adults who might gain a diagnosis of ARFID show more obsessive-compulsive traits and score more highly on measures of disgust, and both children and adults with ARFID also seem to have more contamination fears in general.

Although DSM mentions a reliance on enteral (tube) feeding, this is not a necessity for many children; nor is it often observed that children with ARFID are underweight. Those children who have been given the foods that they like will have been able to take the calories that they need to grow well. It is only where preferred foods have been withheld that the child is likely to show growth faltering. However, if the child does not take any foods which provide dietary iron, appetite is likely to decrease and weight loss will occur; tube feeding might be necessary in the short term for such a child.

Similarly, children with ARFID don't always show any nutritional deficiencies when their diet is assessed by a dietitian; quite often the foods that are accepted (such as dry cereals) are, luckily, fortified or enriched with vitamins and minerals.

Fortified and enriched foods

'Fortified' and 'enriched' both mean that nutrients have been added to make the food more nutritious. *Enriched* means that nutrients lost during food processing have been added back – for example, adding back vitamins lost in the processing of wheat to make white flour. *Fortified* means vitamins or minerals have been added to a food that weren't originally in the food – for example, adding vitamin D to milk or yoghurt.

Some examples are:

- *Bread* – particularly 'branded' versions (rather than a supermarket version). Often contains additional folic acid, iron, B complex vitamins (e.g. thiamine, riboflavin and niacin).

- *Breakfast cereal or cereal bars* – particularly 'branded' cereal products. Often contains additional folic acid, iron, B complex vitamins (see above), calcium, vitamin D.

- *Yoghurt/fromage frais* – often contains additional vitamin D and calcium.

Differential diagnoses?

Some children might get to the second year of life and look as if they have ARFID. They have a very limited diet and, because they are in the neophobic stage, they are often reluctant to try new foods. But not all children with a limited diet are necessarily 'avoidant', with a possible ARFID diagnosis. Some babies have had such a limited experience with food in the first years of life that they have not learned a preference for a good dietary range.

So how do we differentiate between children who have an acquired selective diet and children with ARFID?

Looking further at the criteria for a diagnosis of ARFID, DSM-5 stipulates that the apparent food refusal should not be seen to be linked to the absence of food or the withholding of available food.

We do know that children who have been fed very few foods in the first year and have missed the sensitive periods for the introduction of tastes and textures will only accept a limited range of foods and/or textures in the second year. So these children who have not had food made available to them at the appropriate time would not receive a diagnosis of ARFID.

Some children may have been raised by parents who themselves have a limited-range diet, although this does not always mean that the parents have themselves caused the problem. Parents who themselves have ARFID do not necessarily cause their child to have ARFID. However, some parents are not able to provide a good varied diet for their babies. This might be because the parent is someone who needs general support in child care. These parents are likely to have offered their baby inappropriate foods throughout infancy.

A health professional suggested to one mother, when advising on the introduction of complementary foods, that she pureed the foods that the mother herself ate. Unfortunately, the health professional did not check what the mother ate, and the mother had not been helped to establish a healthy diet for herself. Her diet consisted of a daily pizza, packets of crisps and biscuits. The mother did as she was told and tried to puree the pizza. The baby was then raised to like a range of yoghurts and jars of baby foods, crisp, chips, biscuits and pizza crusts. Once these learned preferences were established, this looked like the diet of a child with ARFID.

Children who have missed out on the early easy period of introduction to foods will often move on more quickly than children who are truly avoidant. They are the children who are more likely to imitate adults and other children when they attend nursery. This is because they:

- are usually not sensory-sensitive and therefore not as anxious about new or different foods

- don't attend so much to the differences between known foods and unknown foods

- don't have such strong disgust responses or high contamination fears

- are also very unlikely to show brand or flavour loyalty – they will eat any kind of digestive biscuit and any flavour yoghurt.

A careful assessment of a child's early history needs to be taken before an ARFID diagnosis can be given, focusing on exposure to foods and indicators of sensory hypersensitivity.

Medically compromised children

Some babies have spent much of their early years struggling with illness, and this has meant that they have been unable to take food orally until their medical condition has resolved. These children may well have been tube-fed for long periods of their early life, either via naso-gastric tubes or via a gastrostomy. Because they have been unable to take solid foods at the best and easiest time for learning about foods, these babies often pass into their second year without being able to accept any textured foods into the mouth.

Usually, they are able to tolerate some pureed or smooth-textured foods, because these might well have been introduced to them in small quantities during their illness. Sometimes, however, no foods have been introduced at all, and the baby is totally reliant upon milk in some form, either from the breast or from a bottle or from a tube feed. If the baby is able to start to try new foods in their second year, then unfortunately they are beginning their journey at the onset of the neophobic period. These children will have a response to food that looks very like the response of children who have started trying food early in life but who have a diagnosis of ARFID. They will have missed out on sensitive and critical periods for the introduction and learned acceptance of solid foods; perhaps the most important of these is the period during which lumpy-textured foods should have been introduced.

> We have seen babies who have been introduced to smooth-textured foods by six months but who then have had to be totally reliant on tube feeding from around 6–12 months because of a medical procedure. These babies were then unable to tolerate any textured food in the mouth when these were introduced in the second year. They were orally defensive and very difficult to move on to solid foods.

These children seem to have a form of acquired ARFID, and they can be just as difficult to move on to a wider range of solid foods as those who receive a diagnosis of ARFID with no medical condition to explain their reaction to food. Again, though, as with children who have had a limited diet in the first year because of parental mealtime strategy, some of these children who have resolved medical conditions will show less extreme food refusal. They will tolerate different brands and flavours of accepted foods and are more ready to imitate other adults and children when they eat.

Just fussy?

How can parents and health professionals tell the difference between those children who are 'just a bit fussy' and those who will gain a diagnosis of ARFID?

This diagnosis becomes easier as the child gets older. The level of distress shown by the child with ARFID at or around mealtimes and food is so extreme that it would be difficult to dismiss the child's reaction as just 'fussy'. In early infancy, however, it is a bit more difficult for parents to work out what is happening and which strategies to use when introducing foods. If the baby spits out a new taste, do you try it again? If they gag on a new lumpy-textured food, do you stop trying with this texture or carry on until they get used to the mouth feel?

Mothers in one study were asked to list foods that they had tried with their babies but which they thought their baby didn't like. When they were supported in offering these foods again to their seven-month-old babies, in small amounts, on alternate days over two weeks, it was found that the babies would eventually happily accept the new foods (Maier *et al.* 2007). In another study, it was found that those mothers who were anxious anyway before they started to offer food to their baby, were more likely to stop offering lumpy-textured food if their baby gagged when it was first offered to them. These babies were more likely to be described at the end of the first year as having feeding problems (Coulthard and Harris 2003). These babies, in both studies, were probably a 'bit fussy', with mothers who were unsure about how to cope with their food refusal behaviour.

Children who are 'just a bit fussy' do have real issues with food, but their reaction is just not as extreme. They may be more sensitive to taste (possibly bitter supertasters), and they are more likely to be slightly sensory-hypersensitive and so need a little more experience with the taste, smell and feel of foods.

Food refusal is on a continuum:

- the higher the sensory sensitivity
- the greater the anxiety
- the less the exposure to foods

then the greater the fear of foods will be.

Messy play, or any activity which means that the child interacts with food in a stress-free way, seems to help fussy children. We have seen that young children who were prompted to touch food, and to rearrange the pieces to copy a picture, were more likely to try the foods later on. We also know that although sensory-hypersensitive children dislike certain textures, slimy foods and food with added 'bits', desensitisation through touch and play will help the child to cope with different textures. Seeing and touching helps with tasting.

Children who are 'fussy', but otherwise have a reasonable dietary range, do then need some help, and messy play is good option with these children.

But do they have ARFID?

Children with the more extreme reaction, at the end of the continuum of hypersensitivity, show more distress when foods that they can't accept are offered to them. And they will go without food for long periods rather than eat a food that they cannot cope with.

I always suggest with 'fussy' babies that a new food, if rejected, should be offered again in small amounts at successive meals. If the baby gets very upset, then stop offering; if the baby is mildly fussed but will take some of the food, then keep offering. Similarly, when offering lumpy-textured foods for the first time, we know that most babies will at first move the food to the back of the tongue and that this will often trigger a gag response. Most babies aren't upset by this and will carry on and try the food again. But those babies who are likely to go on to gain a diagnosis of ARFID are more likely to be extremely distressed at these early stages of the introduction of food; they get very upset with new tastes and textured foods. They will refuse foods that have triggered a gag response.

Offering new foods to a baby who is likely to develop ARFID can be very stressful both for the parent and for the baby. The response to food is far more marked than in other children, and the baby becomes far more distressed in the early years of introduction. Although we might say that the ARFID response is an extension of the neophobic response, extreme behaviours are often noted early on. When taking a history from parents with children who would subsequently meet the criteria for ARFID, most parents would report that the problems really started at around seven months with the introduction of textured foods, with some parents saying that it started earlier with the introduction of tastes, and only a few saying that everything was fine until the child reached the neophobic stage at around the age of two years. But whenever it started, the behaviour of a baby or toddler who might eventually be given a diagnosis of ARFID is so extreme that the usual strategies for introducing new foods just do not work.

Summary

- Some children have extreme problems with food acceptance, and normal strategies used to get them to eat just don't work.

- These children could be diagnosed as having avoidant and restrictive food intake disorder (ARFID).

- Children diagnosed with this eating disorder tend to eat a very limited range of foods and to be sensory-hypersensitive.

- Problems with feeding children with this disorder are often noted at the introduction of solid foods.

- These children then develop extreme neophobia, disgust responses and often contamination fears.

- These children do not imitate the eating behaviours of others around them.

- A child with a diagnosis of ARFID is also more likely to be diagnosed with autism.

- Some other children do still have a very restricted diet when they get into their second year, but this could be because that the child hasn't been exposed to foods in early life. This could be due to:
  - parental management – only a limited range of foods has ever been offered
  - medical problems which have prevented the introduction of solid foods in a timely way in the first year of life.
- 'Fussy' eating behaviour can be seen in children who would not be given a diagnosis of ARFID and these children are likely to be more neophobic and show higher levels of sensory hypersensitivity.
- 'Fussiness' can be mild or extreme, but it still poses problems for the parent.

. . .

Tips for parents and carers

- If your baby shows a strong negative reaction to the first foods offered to them then:
  - offer tastes which are more likely to be easily accepted – sweet and salt, then sour
  - offer a small spoonful each day. If your baby is very distressed, then try another taste; if they just pull a face, then keep on going
  - offer bite-and-dissolve and bite-and-melt textures as first solid foods to babies who seem to gag frequently on lumpy solids
  - avoid giving pureed food with 'bits' in. This is the most difficult texture for a baby to cope with
  - desensitise with messy play whenever possible!

- If your child is mildly fussy, then think about what it is that they have problems with. Tastes? Textures? Mixed foods? Try to cater whenever you can to their needs, but model good eating behaviour yourself. Sit with them and eat. Whenever possible, get them to touch and interact with foods that they are wary of.
- For those who have a child who might receive a diagnosis of ARFID, go to Part 2 of the book!

. . .

Part 2

Avoidant and Restrictive Eating
Strategies and Interventions

Introduction to Part 2

We often tell parents in clinic that for children with avoidant and restrictive eating the usual rules do not apply and that we have to write our own. The second half of this book is exactly that and is a combination of decades of practice-based evidence and academic research. Not least, it is derived from the thousands of young people and their parents who have attended clinic, come to a conference or parent group and given us the wisdom of their experience. For that we thank them; who better to tell us what works and, perhaps more importantly, what doesn't!

The interventions described in the following chapters are suitable for children and teenagers who have features of or a diagnosis of ARFID (described in Chapter 6). As we have already seen, there are different groups of children who might receive this diagnosis. Some develop relatively typically, whereas others show a different developmental pattern, predominantly autism.

We now know that what links these groups is the tendency to display sensory hypersensitivity and associated neophobic, disgust and anxiety responses around foods. These are the factors that both cause and maintain the eating pattern, and addressing these forms the basis for all the intervention ideas that are covered in subsequent chapters. Where there are particular and additional issues for autistic children, these will also be addressed. In all cases, the starting point is to begin from where each child is currently at in terms of what they are eating.

Part 2 of this book begins with two chapters that set the scene for child- and family-specific strategies. Chapter 7 focuses on managing the environment around a child and includes the impact of parental anxiety and stress and school policies on eating. Chapter 8 covers how to know when a child is ready to move on and includes issues such as oral-motor skills and willingness to try a new food. The next three chapters cover particular strategies in more detail, starting in Chapter 9 with what doesn't work and why. Chapters 10 and 11 cover interventions for younger and older children respectively. Lastly, Chapter 12 looks at how to support young people, predominantly those with a diagnosis of autism, who have particularly complex eating patterns.

Chapter 7

Managing the Environment around the Child

Whatever the age of the child, or the extent of their ARFID, there is always an intervention that should work. We hope that is reassuring to the parents reading this! However, what will work is often dependent on factors in the environment around the child. Influences such as parental or family anxiety and what happens at school are all crucial and, if not addressed, can affect the success of any intervention. Of course, this does not mean that this eating pattern is the fault of parents, carers or schools, – quite the opposite. It is rather that these wider problems or barriers need to be addressed at the start of any intervention plan in order to set the scene for more child- and family-specific strategies.

Parental and family anxiety

There is probably no more frustrating a parenting task than trying to feed, or cook for, a fussy and reluctant infant, toddler, child or teenager. Each of these developmental stages brings its own refusal behaviours, ranging from the infant who clamps their mouth firmly shut at the approach of the spoon or who simply screams, to the child who hides their breakfast behind the sofa and the teenager who refuses to come out of their bedroom to attend a family party. Add on the daily tasks of managing autism, if present, and family life in general, and it is no wonder that many parents arrive in clinic feeling overwhelmed and confused about how best to manage mealtimes.

For these parents, feelings of worry, anxiety, panic and even despair are common, as are feelings of failure and a lack of confidence in parenting ability in general. If you are a parent reading this, it is very important for you to know that these are all typical and entirely understandable feelings. All parents report feeling this way when their child is an avoidant eater. What's more, these feelings arise from the most common fears parents express about their child's eating:

- Will my child starve?

- Will they get ill?

- Will they suffer in the long term?

Not only are these fears very powerful, but for many parents they are also present on a daily basis – not surprising given that mealtimes happen, on average, at least three times a day! It is hard to think of any other part of being a parent that so regularly causes so much stress and confusion.

What we do know, from decades of meeting families with children with avoidant eating and restricted diets, is that the vast majority of them grow well, do not have any nutritional deficiencies and are healthy. However, we still do not fully know why this is, although, as we have already seen, the majority of them take in the right amount of calories and many foods accepted by these children are fortified. Again, we hope this is reassuring for parents. However, if you are a parent who is still worried about any aspect of your child's health in relation to their eating, then do not hesitate to seek a referral to a relevant health professional. Table 7.1 provides a list of health professionals who work with childhood eating problems and what they can provide.

Table 7.1 Health professionals who work with childhood eating problems

Health professional	Works with	Helps to
Clinical psychologist	Behaviour, emotional, psychological and/or mental health issues	Reduce anxiety, teach relaxation and manage mealtime stress
Dietician	Nutrition and growth	Monitor growth and check dietary range
Gastroenterologist	Gut and bowel issues – e.g. constipation, diarrhoea, allergies/ intolerances	Prescribe medications and conduct physical examinations
Hypnotherapist	Phobias, anxiety and other mental health issues	Teach relaxation/ visualisation
Occupational therapist	Tasks of daily living, sensory issues	Assess and intervene with oral-motor skills and sensory issues
Paediatrician	Child health conditions	Monitor growth, health/development and coordinate with/ refer to other services
Speech and language therapist	Communication, eating and swallowing skills	Assess chewing and swallowing, provide sensory/ desensitisation programmes

Feelings of blame

For many parents, this confusion about what they should be doing to help their child eat well comes not only from their own anxiety and a lack of confidence about how best to manage mealtimes, but also from the huge amount of advice out there about feeding children. From well-meaning family and friends to information in the media, it seems everyone has an opinion about how best to approach a 'fussy' child.

Although there is accessible, practical and helpful advice out there, unfortunately there is also much that is contradictory, inappropriate and unhelpful, sometimes even when it comes from health professionals! This just contributes to the growing sense of anxiety in the parent and can result in them feeling as if it must be their fault. Almost without exception, every parent who comes to clinic feels they are somehow to blame for their child's eating difficulties. If you are a parent reading this, you are likely to be no different.

Why do parents blame themselves?

Feeding children, and therefore keeping them alive, is the single most important task of being a parent. If this goes wrong, for whatever reason, it is natural to look for reasons why. Although there may be very definite and obvious reasons for a feeding problem, such as a serious illness, parents still tend to place the blame firmly at their own door. So, even when a parent knows it is not their fault, these feelings of blame and the associated guilt when the child doesn't eat are very persistent.

It is also common for parents to disagree about how to feed an avoidant child. In clinic we often find one parent has already adopted the strategy of allowing the preferred foods, but the other is still insisting the child eats 'healthier' options. In addition, it is also common for children with ARFID to eat different foods for different people. For example, the child will accept a food cooked a specific way by a particular relative but not that same food cooked by a parent who perhaps does not cook it quite 'right'. This can be particularly true for those on the autism spectrum. This is because it is not just the foods and the packaging that predict the safety, but sometimes also the context the foods are eaten in. Unfortunately, this may be misunderstood as somehow being the fault of the parent and comments by well-meaning friends and family such as 'Well, they eat that at my house' can make a parent feel even more to blame.

The same can also be true of professionals who can, again without meaning to, end up blaming the parent. This is more likely to be the case if the professional hasn't come across a child with ARFID before and does not recognise the eating pattern or know how to deal with it. Unfortunately, this can get worse where there are several professionals involved and it is common for the parent to be given conflicting advice. It can also get worse when a parent has their own issues with food, mental health or general parenting and, in the absence of a good understanding of ARFID, these are labelled as the reason the child doesn't eat well. It is no wonder that many parents feel responsible for their child's eating problem and carry a great deal of guilt.

Blaming the parent

Louisa is 15 and has autism and some learning difficulties. Her mother, Anne, became very worried when Louisa began to lose weight. This followed Louisa transferring to a different classroom within her school. As a younger child, Louisa had refused lumpy foods, had always had a limited diet and ate within very specific and rigid routines. However, until recently she had maintained her weight. Social Services became concerned at her weight loss and began to monitor her closely.

During this time Anne disclosed to her social worker that she herself suffered from bouts of anxiety and had always struggled with her eating, so much so that as a teenager she had been labelled 'anorexic'. The social worker then began to suggest that Anne was deliberately restricting Louisa's foods because she didn't want Louisa to get 'fat'. Although Anne knew this was not the case, it was very evident that she blamed herself for Louisa's eating pattern, saying that Louisa must have learnt her issues with food from herself.

Observation at home and at school revealed that Louisa had ARFID and had only begun to lose weight after the change to routines in school. This had led to anxiety and Louisa refusing even her most preferred foods. Giving the diagnosis of ARFID meant Anne no longer felt to blame and her social worker understood Louisa's eating pattern. What's more, further discussion revealed that Anne's own pattern of eating was very similar to Louisa's, and that the diagnosis of ARFID may also explain her eating behaviour. Once Louisa settled into the new classroom, she began to eat her usual foods again and her weight picked up.

The impact of anxiety, blame and guilt

An anxious and guilt-ridden parent will do almost anything to ensure that their child eats. This is understandable and many parents reading this will probably have already tried (or perhaps been advised by a professional to try) one or more of the following:

- Persuading and coaxing the child to eat.

- Bribing or rewarding the child.

- Withholding a preferred food until another food is eaten.

- Hiding or disguising a new food in a preferred food.

- Making the child sit at the table until a food is eaten.

- Leaving the child to 'go hungry' until they eat.

- Forcing the child to eat a food.

Perhaps these sound like common sense? However, if you have tried any of these strategies with a child with ARFID, then you will know they simply do not work. In fact, instead of increasing the amount or the range of food the child eats, they are more likely to reduce what the child eats and make family life at mealtimes much more stressful. Remember that for children with ARFID, we need a new 'rule book'.

We will cover why these strategies don't work in more detail in Chapter 9. For now, if you have used any of these as a parent, or recommended them as a professional, then don't blame yourself! You are reading this book because you want to learn what does work and you are prepared to put some time into finding out.

Why we shouldn't blame parents

As you will hear many times throughout this book, the first and most important intervention in ARFID is to allow the child to have their preferred foods, whatever these are and in all locations. Doing so results in the majority of children growing as expected and staying healthy.

The eating behaviours we see in ARFID are due to particular developmental traits, such as sensory hypersensitivity, neophobia and disgust. They do not occur because of what parents have done or not done. This is a fundamental concept to grasp, both for parents themselves and, crucially, for professionals. In fact, it is perhaps the single most powerful intervention in a professional's tool-kit. Telling a parent that they are not to blame for their child's eating problems can instantly transform that parent to feel more capable, confident and in control of mealtimes.

A good understanding of ARFID is therefore crucial for professionals as well as families. Taking the time to listen to a family's concerns, and then taking these seriously, is the first step to moving on. A parent who does not feel to blame and is reassured is a parent who is able to follow an intervention plan.

. . .

Tips for professionals

- Understand the eating patterns seen in ARFID.
- Listen to parents and take their concerns seriously.
- Reassure parents that the eating pattern is not their fault.
- Consult with colleagues to make sure consistent advice is given.

. . .

Eating in school

School is a very important and often positive part of any child's life. However, it can also be challenging, particularly for those who have problems eating. It is very common for children with ARFID to struggle to eat and/or drink well at school. A combination of different routines, sensory 'overload' and a lack of availability of the child's preferred foods can all lead to an increase in the child's anxiety and a reduced intake. This can mean that the child is at risk of going the whole day without eating or drinking. This can have an associated impact on the child's weight, growth, health, energy levels, learning ability and general development. Interventions for managing routines and sensory overload will be covered in Chapters 10 and 11. For now, let's concentrate on what schools can do, in a wider context, to remove the barriers to the child eating well there.

'Healthy eating' policies

Allowing the child's preferred foods, whatever these are, should also be applied in schools. However, making sure that the child's preferred foods are available frequently presents considerable challenges for parents and schools alike. There has been a significant rise in obesity in children in the UK which has long-term health and social consequences. Current (at the time of press) UK government guidance on obesity encourages schools to make the availability of healthy foods a priority, particularly for younger children. As a result, many schools are under pressure to universally adopt 'heathy eating' policies. These can range from a complete ban on children bringing their own food into school to a ban on foods considered to be 'unhealthy' (think chocolate, crisps or biscuits).

Although these are, of course, admirable policies designed to reduce the risk of children becoming overweight, it is rare to meet any child with ARFID who is happy having school dinners or who eats a piece of fruit at snack time. In fact, it is more common for these children not to eat in school simply because the foods that are available are not foods they can accept. This, of course, has a number of negative consequences including reducing the overall amount and range of foods the child is able to eat, limiting their opportunities for active participation during meal and snack times, and potentially having an impact on their concentration and learning potential during the school day. For autistic children in particular, many of these areas are already significantly affected by their social and cognitive differences.

In addition, it is more common for children with ARFID to be at risk of becoming underweight rather than overweight, and as a result they need regular eating opportunities, particularly during the school day. What's more, many of these children may be slow eaters and not have enough time at lunch to finish their food, or they may only eat small amounts at snack and mealtimes.

No such thing as 'junk food'

For a child with avoidant eating there is no such thing as 'junk food'. Remember, these children are more at risk of losing weight than gaining it! In fact, for many reasons (poor appetite recognition, sensory hypersensitivity and high anxiety) these children benefit from what we call in clinic 'high calorie per mouthful' foods. Good examples of these are chocolate, biscuits, crisps, cake or a cereal bar. These are foods that the child can eat in relatively small amounts but gain a good calorie load from. These foods are particularly good for children who eat slowly, who only eat small amounts in one sitting or who are very anxious during the school day. These foods should be offered at scheduled snack and lunch times.

A new 'rule book' for schools

This, of course, does not mean that schools are unsupportive or unresponsive to children's eating difficulties – quite the opposite. It simply means that schools are subject to wider social and health policies, which do not always take into account those children who need alternative support. So what alternative strategies can schools adopt instead? Establishing good communication with parents and allowing the child's preferred foods within school are the key.

For a child with ARFID, good communication between home and school about what the child is eating and drinking is crucial. This is particularly true if the child is on the autism spectrum and is not verbal. When a child is due to start nursery, reception or secondary school, or even at the start of each school year, it is a good idea for parents and school staff to meet. This meeting could focus on discussing the child's eating pattern, their current dietary range and whether there are any particular eating behaviours that need to be monitored or managed.

For children who find eating and/or drinking in school difficult, a home–school food diary can be very useful. This is also a useful tool to use routinely with non-verbal autistic children.

The diary can record the child's preferred foods, their preferred eating routines and what the child has eaten before or during school (both of which can have an impact on the child's behaviour during the day or after school). This can be very helpful if the child eats different foods at home and at school. A diary also helps parents track the overall amounts a child has eaten over the day. This is particularly important if there are concerns about weight, growth or nutrition.

We have already emphasised the importance of allowing a child's preferred range of foods in order to maintain their weight, growth pattern and general health. This is perhaps even more important in school, ensuring as it does that the ARFID child has the best chance of meeting their learning and social potential. It can be done simply by allowing the child to take in a 'snack/lunch' box containing a selection of their safe and preferred foods. They should then be allowed access to these foods during the school day and/or at scheduled snack and lunch times. It is very important that only accepted foods go in the box. Putting in new, different or unaccepted foods will not encourage the child to eat them. Rather, it is more likely that these foods will 'contaminate' the preferred foods (see Chapters 4 and 9 for more information on contamination). Using a box with separate compartments is a good idea for children who do not like any of their preferred foods touching.

Lastly, many children with ARFID experience sensory 'overload' in busy eating environments such as a school dining room. Chapter 10 will discuss sensory overload in more detail. However, it is worth saying here that simply allowing the ARFID child to eat their lunch in school away from overpowering sights, smells or noises can improve their intake significantly.

Allowing preferred foods in school

Poppy displayed many sensory issues around foods from an early age and received an ARFID diagnosis at the age of four. She frequently gagged or vomited at the sight or smell of foods she didn't eat and would refuse anything that looked slightly different from usual.

When she started school, her parents were told that Poppy would need to have the same fruit snack as the other children and have school dinners. Unfortunately, Poppy couldn't cope with the sights and smells of the school dining room and would vomit or retch. She wasn't able to eat the available foods at snack or at lunch and she began to lose weight. At the same time Poppy started to tell her parents she was 'ill' and couldn't go to school.

Poppy's parents approached the school and explained her eating pattern. This led to her being allowed to take her own foods in for snack and lunch. She was also allowed to eat her lunch in the classroom instead of the dining room. The vomiting stopped, and soon Poppy's attendance and weight were back to normal.

It is important that schools in particular are aware that ARFID is now a recognised diagnosis and that, as such, children with this eating pattern are entitled to have their needs met in school. Simple changes such as allowing a child's accepted foods and providing an alternative to the dining room can go a long way to improving a child's eating during the school day.

. . .

Tips for schools

- Allow the child's safe and accepted/preferred foods at snack and lunch times.
- Meet with parents regularly to review the child's eating.

- Monitor the child's intake with a home–school food diary.
- Rebrand! For children with ARFID, there is no such thing as 'junk food'.
- Allow the child, if necessary, to eat in a quiet location away from others.

. . .

Summary

- Feelings of worry, anxiety, blame and guilt are all common parental reactions to a child with ARFID.

- Parents who are anxious will often use extreme strategies to get their child to eat. Unfortunately, these often make the eating pattern worse.

- Telling a parent that they are not to blame enables them to feel less anxious, more capable and more in control of mealtimes.

- Allowing the child to have their preferred foods, whatever these are and in all locations, typically results in the child growing as expected and being generally healthy.

- Healthy eating policies in schools can result in reducing the opportunities for a child with ARFID to eat well and potentially affects their learning and social potential.

- Good communication with parents, allowing access to a child's preferred foods and allowing them to eat away from others are alternative strategies that schools can use to improve a child's intake during the school day.

. . .

Tips for parents and carers

- Understand that your child's eating pattern is not your fault but has happened because of their ARFID. Don't blame yourself!
- Allow your child's preferred foods; this maintains weight, growth, health and nutrition.
- Explain ARFID to other family members.
- Explain to other family members what they can do to support you and your child. This might include what *not* to do!
- Explain ARFID to your child's school. Ask them to support strategies you are using at home and to communicate with you about what your child is eating (and how) in school.

. . .

Chapter 8

Is the Child Ready to Move On?

Where have we got to?

In the previous chapter we saw the importance of the environment around the child and, in particular, how resolving anxiety in parents and carers and barriers in school can help a child with ARFID to eat better. Once these have been tackled, perhaps the single most important factor in determining both what intervention to use and its likely success is whether the child is ready. Readiness to move on includes where the child is in terms of what textures they can tolerate and eat, and their willingness to try a different food. The chapter will end with some ideas about what to expect once you start an intervention.

Tolerating texture

Many families come to clinic concerned about their child's restricted range of foods and, as a result, want them to start to eat new or different foods. As we saw in Chapter 7, this is usually because they are worried about the amount the child is eating or the impact of a restricted diet on health and nutrition. All of this is understandable, and it seems like a sensible goal to want the child to eat something new and different. Choosing and introducing a new food is covered in detail in Chapters 10 and 11. However, it is worth discussing the first step here: how do we know the child is ready to tolerate and cope with the food from a sensory point of view?

We have already discussed how children learn to like the foods they eat. Through the first year of life the baby is exposed to smells, tastes and textures. For all children there are some tastes and textures that are hard to acquire, such as a bitter taste – for example, broccoli – or a slimy texture – for example, mushrooms (see Chapter 1). Taste and smell preferences are frequently reported in children with ARFID, and interventions for these will be covered in Chapters 10 and 11. However, it is often difficulties with textured foods in the mouth, and the impact of these on the child's oral-motor skills, that can prevent the child from moving on.

Texture sensitivity

As we have seen already in Chapter 1, learning to cope with food textures in the mouth and learning to chew are an essential part of the process of moving from a liquid (milk) diet to eating solid foods. Most children will successfully master this by the age of two years. However, if these skills are not acquired by the baby during the 'critical' period (thought to be between 6 and 10 months of age), then it becomes much harder for the baby to learn them later on. This generally results in long-lasting difficulties with tolerating the feel of textures in the mouth and being able to chew.

Common difficulties that arise at this stage of learning about foods are touch or 'tactile' sensory differences. Frequently, these are present at birth but perhaps only become obvious when the child is offered foods with harder-to-manage textures. We often see children in clinic, for example, who have coped well with first-stage weaning foods (smooth purees) but struggled when the foods became more textured or lumpy. These children have a touch or tactile 'hypersensitivity' and this is often when parents of ARFID children say the problem with feeding began. Sensory differences in general are core to the diagnosis of ARFID, and also of autism, and are included in the diagnostic criteria for both of these conditions.

A child with a tactile hypersensitivity will often 'over-respond' to the sensation of touch and can therefore find the experience of having particular textures in the mouth very aversive. So much so that solid foods are refused at their first presentation and the child does not then learn the oral-motor skills necessary to manage them, either early on or in later childhood. This means that some ARFID children do not progress beyond the pureed weaning stage, or may even remain stuck on milk diets throughout their childhood. This does not mean they have medical problems with chewing or swallowing (termed 'dysphagia'). Instead, they have an intense reaction to the feel of certain textures in the mouth. This appears to be particularly prevalent in autistic children, who often present with very extreme sensory sensitivities.

> For Rebecca, who has ARFID and Asperger's syndrome, even a tiny amount of a food which is the wrong texture (or just the thought of it) caused her extreme anxiety and disgust.
>
> > My favourite food is chocolate crispy cake, I only like them when they are melted. I only like crunchy things. I wouldn't want to try new foods, because they might make me sick. At birthdays I have a cake, and I make a wish and blow out the candles, but I never try it. I once had a tiny crumb of birthday cake, but it made me feel sick. (Rebecca, age 13)

As we have already seen in Chapter 3, as sensory sensitivity increases, so do feelings of anxiety and awareness or 'vigilance' to changes in foods. So we can see for ARFID children that sensory sensitivity really is the key.

Many ARFID children with texture sensitivity choose which foods to eat depending on the texture. For some these are crispy, crunchy and predominantly dry foods. For others, particularly where there are delays in their oral-motor skills, this means a reliance on liquid, smooth or pureed foods. This is because these can be easily managed and swallowed. Being able to identify what stage of texture acceptance the child is currently at really helps when choosing the appropriate first steps in intervention. For example, it helps in the decision about what to 'wean' a child on to in the next texture stage, such as from smooth purees to thicker textures, or foods that bite and dissolve.

Moving on with texture

Callum, aged 8, has autism and a learning disability. He drinks milk from a baby bottle and eats two flavours of custard and one flavour of one brand of pureed baby food. As a baby he gagged at lumpier foods and has refused anything but smooth-textured foods and milk since. Recently, the manufacturer of the baby food has changed the recipe, and Callum is now refusing to eat it. His parents decided to use the opportunity of the loss of the baby food to try to move him on. Instead, they are offering him foods which melt in the mouth easily such as chocolate buttons (one of his custard pots was already chocolate-flavoured) and some bite-and-dissolve crisps. Callum was initially reluctant but after a few exposures he is now happily eating the new foods.

Food choices

Over the years, we have learnt which foods sensory-sensitive children will eat. In fact, it is often so easy to predict the foods that are most likely to be eaten that children in clinic are always impressed that we know what foods they eat before they or their parents tell us! Table 8.1 details the most common categories of foods accepted by ARFID children and some of the typical behaviours around foods, and what this tells us about their sensory sensitivities.

Table 8.1 Common categories of accepted foods and sensory sensitivity

Food category/behaviour	Sensory sensitivity?
Beige carbohydrate foods, e.g. bread, cereal, biscuits, pasta, chips	Texture sensitivity – dry and/or crispy Visual sensitivity – appearance, e.g. toast has to be the right shade of brown Taste sensitivity – only eating one brand/flavour
Smooth, single-textured foods, e.g. smooth yoghurt, custard, fruit puree	Texture sensitivity – contain no surprise 'bits' and are easily processed in the mouth
Smooth chocolate, e.g. milk chocolate, buttons, chocolate icing	Texture sensitivity – melt in the mouth at body temperature and are easily processed in the mouth
Bite-and-dissolve foods, e.g. melt-in-the-mouth crisps, wafer biscuit	Texture sensitivity – these foods dissolve in the mouth without the need for much chewing
Processed foods, e.g. chicken nuggets, sausage	Texture sensitivity – these foods are 'pre-chewed' (during the processing) and are therefore easier to process in the mouth Visual sensitivity – these foods are usually branded
Branded foods, e.g. fast-food restaurants, popular manufacturers	Visual sensitivity – the brand and the packaging predict the safety of the food Taste sensitivity – if very brand-loyal
Avoidance of mealtimes, e.g. not eating at school in the dining room	Auditory (noise) sensitivity Smell sensitivity and/or disgust – at other people's foods/sight of others eating Sensory 'overload' – eating is avoided altogether
Refusing foods that look similar but have something added, e.g. vitamins added to a drink	Smell sensitivity – will be noticed and rejected

In addition to the clues that the food choices of tactile-sensitive (sometimes also termed 'tactile-defensive') children give us, it is often easy to spot a child with delays in their oral-motor skills, even without a formal assessment. These are children who don't chew at the sides of their mouth, perhaps trying instead to chew at the front or frequently gagging on foods they have tried to swallow too soon. These are also the children who hate to have their teeth cleaned. For these children, a referral to a speech and language therapist who can assess the child's oral-motor skills can be very useful. Such an assessment should also lead to further intervention to help the child slowly learn to tolerate and cope with different textures in the mouth. This is called 'desensitisation' and will be discussed in more detail in Chapters 10 and 11, along with other sensory strategies.

Exclusive milk diets

Often tactile hypersensitive children rely on milk for a proportion of their daily calorie needs. Sometimes the child hasn't progressed to other textures at all, or has regressed as he or she has got older and is now stuck on an entirely liquid diet, usually milk. These children, who are, in effect, still in the very early stages of food acceptance or 'pre-weaning', represent the extreme end of a texture-sensitive spectrum. They also tend to avoid contact with wet or sticky textures on their hands (and hate messy play) and don't like food around their mouth or on their face. They may have been able to accept some purees during weaning but could not accept the more textured second stage of weaning foods which were aversive to them. Over time, this aversion has generalised to any food other than milk. In this respect, ARFID children stuck on milk diets are similar to other children who are tube-fed or on 'supplementary', high-calorie feeds.

Unfortunately, avoidant children are often happy to stay on their milk, supplementary or tube feeds and see no reason for moving on. This is because they are so reluctant to try new foods and have so many problems with the acceptance of tastes and textures. In addition, they have more problems with managing appetite in general and are often more rigid and routine-bound around foods and mealtimes than other children. This is why tube feeding or supplementary foods should be avoided for an ARFID child wherever possible.

Stimulating appetite

For all children on any form of milk or supplemented diet, a 'hunger provocation' programme may be necessary. This involves making a gradual reduction in the amount of milk or supplement that is given daily in order to stimulate the child's appetite. The child can then be offered another food which is of a similar calorie load to the amount of the milk reduction and is of a texture they can cope with. A hunger provocation programme can only be done if the reason for the tube or supplement is no longer there (e.g. the child has recovered from a previous illness or medical issue), the child has a safe swallow and the child's height and weight are stable. Such a programme should always be done with the support and supervision of appropriate health professionals, such as a dietician who can monitor weight or a speech and language or occupational therapist who can work with the sensory issues.

Can the child swallow safely?
For all children who have been exclusively milk-fed, past the usual weaning periods, it is essential that their chewing and swallowing skills are assessed before a hunger provocation programme begins – in particular, to ensure the child can swallow safely, and there are no risks of choking or 'aspiration' (swallowing food into the lungs), both of which can have serious consequences. Such an assessment is usually carried out by a speech and language therapist qualified in the assessment of dysphagia, the medical term for swallowing difficulties.

Willingness to try a new food

In addition to whether the child is ready to move on in their acceptance of textures, one of our most important assessments in clinic is working out whether the child is ready to try a new food. Some common signs that a child with ARFID may be ready to do this include:

- showing an interest in what others are eating, particularly peers

- accepting a different flavour or brand of a preferred food

- asking for a new food

- eating something new spontaneously.

The point at which a child reaches the stage of being willing to try a new or different food is determined by how motivated they are and their age. These will vary depending on the individual child and the extent to which their ARFID, and autism if relevant, affects them.

Motivation

The more motivated a child with ARFID is, the easier it will be for them to move on. This is because motivation helps to overcome anxiety. Common examples of motivation in children with ARFID include wanting to go somewhere specific to eat, going on a school trip or family holiday and wanting to eat a particular food, perhaps because it has a particular significance.

> Thomas, aged 11, wants to go on a school trip to France and is working on trying to eat a baguette, so that he will be able to eat it while he is there. Similarly, Charlie's family are going to New York for his 18th birthday, and he is determined to learn how to eat hamburgers before he goes.

Both of these young people are likely to find trying these new foods anxiety-provoking, at least to begin with. However, because they are motivated, it will be easier for them to learn and apply strategies for lowering their anxiety. Motivation also increases with age. We have found that many autistic teenagers with ARFID, despite their social differences, do want to fit in with their peers and become more willing to try a food that their friends eat as they get older.

> Rebecca, who has ARFID and Asperger's syndrome, wants a sleepover for her birthday but is worried her

friends will think she is 'weird' if she has chocolate and crisps for breakfast. She has decided she would like to work on trying toast as this is a 'good' breakfast food and one her friends also eat.

For the older and more able age group, motivation is the key to success. We will return to it in Chapter 11, where we will explain how to introduce a new or different food to a motivated child or teenager, and, in particular, how to work with anxiety.

Getting older

The older a child with ARFID gets, the more likely they will be able to try something new. This is because motivation to change increases with age and older children and teenagers have developed the 'cognitive' (thinking) skills necessary to help them overcome their fears.

As we have already seen, children without ARFID typically move into the neophobic stage in the second year of life and come out of it during the pre-school years by imitating others eating. It is not so much that children have to overcome their early fear, rather that it gradually lessens as they learn which foods are safe and okay to eat. However, for children with ARFID, who are not as influenced by others eating, this fear remains fixed and appears to worsen during early childhood. These fears will also get worse if well-meaning family, friends or teachers continue to try to persuade the avoidant child to eat something different!

For these children, it is not until middle childhood (typically aged 8 and above) that we see some change in their willingness to move on. This willingness starts as a gradual and natural shift in the child's attitude towards foods and eating and in their ability to control their fears.

> William is 9 and has ARFID. To date, he has shown very little willingness to try anything new, much to the frustration of his family. However, during the last school term he has tried some cheese during a French lesson and ate a different variety of chicken nuggets at a friend's house.

Some children, however, who have a milder form of ARFID, will show signs that they can move on gradually from an earlier age than this, perhaps at around five years of age. This is when most children are moving out of the neophobic stage. For these children, interventions such as 'spreading the sets' (see Chapter 10) will be helpful.

However, for autistic children and teenagers, the age at which natural change begins, or where some interventions become possible, is more individual and depends upon the extent to which their autism impacts on them. For these children, it is a good idea to work out the child's 'developmental age'. This is a guide to what they will be able to cope with on a daily basis, including how independent they are and the level of their social and emotional skills.

Working out the 'developmental age'

Some years ago a colleague of mine gave me a good 'rule of thumb' to work out the developmental age of an autistic child or teenager:

- If the child has no learning disability or developmental delay, then subtract approximately one-third from their chronological age to get to their developmental age – e.g. if the child's chronological age is 12, their developmental age is around 8.

- If the child has a learning disability or developmental delay, consider other factors, such as how independent they are in daily skills such as dressing or going to the toilet. Estimate the child's developmental age based on their level of independence – e.g. a child with a chronological age of 12 who is not yet toilet trained may therefore have a developmental age somewhere in the pre-school years.

(Dr Stephanie Boyle, personal communication)

It is the child's developmental age that tells us when they might be ready to move on with foods. So, for example, we might see a natural shift in food behaviour occurring in an autistic 12- or 13-year-old, rather than at the age of 8 or 9 in a child with ARFID but without autism. Working out what the child can cope with in this way also helps us manage our expectations once an intervention has begun.

Managing expectations

We will end this chapter by discussing what to expect once a child is identified as being 'ready'. I often find in clinic that once I have assessed the child's eating and given a diagnosis of ARFID, the level of motivation in the parents for the child to move on is very high indeed! That is a positive step and comes, no doubt, from the fact that the eating pattern and the stress associated with it are being taken seriously by a health professional, perhaps for the first time.

However, ARFID has usually been around for a long time (the average age for a diagnosis of ARFID in our clinic is around 12) and overcoming the sensory issues, disgust and anxiety is not an easy task. In addition, any change in a child's eating pattern has to be given time to settle in and adjust to, particularly if it involves a new routine or food. Progress with any intervention can therefore be slow. Remember, it takes approximately ten tastes for anyone older than the age of two to learn to like a new food and for the brain to adjust to that change. Similarly, if we are reducing a reliance on a milk diet, this can take many months.

> Mia, aged 6, has ARFID, autism and a learning disability. She only drinks formula milk and one brand of strawberry milkshake made with cow's milk. Following professional advice, Mia's parents slowly reduced her milk intake and at the same time introduced a strawberry-flavoured smooth yoghurt and some melt-in-the-mouth textures. Given that she was entirely dependent on her milk feeds at the start, and each reduction was small in order to allow Mia to get used to the change and to minimise the risk of

her losing weight, her parents knew they were in for
many months of intervention.

In our experience, once families have a plan, that really helps
them to stay positive and for motivation to remain high. Patience
also helps! This is no bad thing given the fact that children with
ARFID, particularly those on the autism spectrum, frequently
need extra time to adjust to changes to any routine. Keeping a
record of any progress, however small, will also help. Remember
that for a child who only eats four foods, one new food is a 25 per
cent increase!

Summary

- Children with ARFID are likely to have hypersensitivity,
  particularly to texture.

- Children with texture hypersensitivity are likely to have
  under-developed oral-motor skills.

- Children with under-developed oral-motor skills often
  stick to particular textures and may not have progressed
  through the usual stages of weaning.

- Working out where the child currently is in terms of
  sensory acceptance, particularly to texture, is the first
  step in moving on.

- Children with texture hypersensitivity benefit from
  starting with the stage of texture acceptance they are
  currently at and gradually moving on to the next – for
  example, from purees to more textured foods.

- Children on exclusive milk diets are likely to need a
  'hunger provocation' approach. This should only be done
  with the input and support of health professionals.

- Readiness to move on includes willingness to try a
  new food.

- Willingness to try a new food is affected by motivation
  and age, both of which are influenced by the child's
  development and extent of their autism and/or learning
  disability if present.

- Any intervention needs time to settle in. Having a plan and being patient are the keys to success.

. . .

Tips for parents and carers

- Look at your child's range of foods. What clues does this give you about where they are in terms of texture acceptance?
- If it is safe to do so, offer foods from the next stage. For example, from a milk diet, offer smooth purees or bite-and-dissolve foods.
- Involve appropriate health professionals, particularly if there are concerns about the safety of your child's chewing and swallowing skills.
- Work out your child's developmental age. This will help you tell whether they ready to try some new foods.
- Look for signs that your child is willing to try a new food. This typically starts around the developmental age of 8 years old.
- Allow yourself to wait if your child is not showing any signs of readiness yet.
- Go at a steady pace, particularly if your child is autistic. These children need more time to adjust to changes to routines.
- Keep a record of your child's progress; this will help you, and them, stay motivated.

. . .

Chapter 9

What Doesn't Work and Why

Where have we got to?

In the previous chapter we learnt that understanding whether the child is ready to move on, either from what they can accept in terms of texture or from their age and level of motivation, is important before starting any intervention. Now we come to perhaps the most important chapter of this book: what doesn't work and why.

> We have tried bribery, mixing foods, threats, rewards, eating in different places and making lists of foods. We have tried having other children around at mealtimes to try to get her to join in, but she doesn't. She stopped eating at school when they tried to insist she ate more. In fact, the more we try to get her to eat, the less she will do it. (Parent of a ten-year-old girl)

Many of you will be familiar with the words of this parent, and perhaps the feelings of frustration that go along with them. Without fail, every time we talk to a group of parents, professionals or a family in clinic we hear a list of the things they have tried that don't work. As a result, I suspect this may also be the most familiar chapter in this book! We started the second half of this book by discussing why parents blame themselves. So if you are a parent who has tried any of these strategies, or a professional who has ever advised any of them, remember: do not blame yourself.

For children with ARFID it seems that practically anything will stop them eating. Learning why is the first step towards understanding what does work. Many of the strategies presented below might seem like common sense and, in fact, may even be recommended for 'just fussy' children. However, remember we are writing our own rule book and part of that has been to make and learn from our collective mistakes along the way.

Pressure to eat

Who hasn't sat with a reluctant toddler and played the train or aeroplane game in order to get a spoon of food in? Who hasn't persuaded, encouraged or even begged a fussy child or teenager to eat a 'healthy' food or to finish their meal? Pressure to eat includes a range of behaviours by adults, from gentle persuasion to forcing the child to eat. All of these are generally driven by the desire to provide adequate nutrition and ever-increasing anxiety if the child refuses. In fact, in our clinical experience, the more anxious a parent is, the more they 'up the ante' in trying to get the child to eat.

How do adults pressurise children to eat?

- *Encouragement* – for example, clapping or cheering when a child eats and giving too much attention to the child at mealtimes.

- *Persuasion or prompting* – comments such as 'Eat up, it tastes lovely' or playing games with food.

- *Guilt* – comments such as 'Eat up, there are starving children in...' or using the adult's own emotional state: 'It will make me happy if you eat.'

- *Sitting in front of a new food* – for example, not letting the child leave the table until the food is eaten.

- *Threats* – comments such as 'If you don't eat, I'll...' or applying punishments or consequences.

- *Forcing* – for example, holding a child down or pushing food in the mouth when the child is crying.

We know from research that it is common for an adult to avoid a food that they were made to eat as a child. When I was a child, my mum made gooseberry crumble. I liked the crumble very much, but the taste and texture of the gooseberry was very unpleasant (sour and grainy). I wasn't allowed to leave the table until I had eaten all the pudding. I sat at the table for over an hour, taking very tiny and reluctant mouthfuls. My mum never gave me gooseberry crumble again, and I've never since eaten a gooseberry! Of course, not every parent will use, or every professional recommend, these more extreme methods of pressuring a child. However, even what seems like gentle persuasion can have an impact on a child's acceptance of a food.

Persuasion to eat

One team of researchers examined whether pressuring young children to eat would affect their food intake and preferences. In the experiment, a group of children were repeatedly told to 'finish your soup', while other children were allowed to eat soup without such persuasion. The children who were told to finish their soup ate less soup than children who were not told to do so, and made more negative comments about the soup, such as, 'I don't want to drink it', 'I hate it' and 'I never will eat my soup' (Galloway et al. 2006). So it seems that when children are prompted or persuaded to eat, rather than improving their intake, it actually does the opposite!

The language we use is also important when talking to children about eating, particularly those on the autism spectrum who may be very literal. One parent I know decided to persuade her son to eat by using his special interest in cars:

Mum: 'You have to eat; you need food just like a car needs petrol.'

Dan: 'I don't need petrol; I'm a diesel car.'

Unfortunately, Mum didn't have an answer to that!

We also need to be careful not to make too much of a fuss when a child with ARFID shows an interest in a new food, where it is usual for the parent to be very excited about the prospect of them eating it. This can be too much for the child to cope with. For example, Oliver, aged 11, decided he wanted to try sausages. Following some work to help him desensitise, Oliver tasted a sausage for the first time during breakfast while on holiday, but no one else in the family noticed, as they were all too busy. Oliver later said he didn't think he could have tried the sausage if everyone had been watching him, as this would have been extra pressure and would have made it much harder. Certainly, when I am working on trying foods with a young person (called 'taste trials' – see Chapter 11), we have the first taste without the parent in the room in order to minimise this extra social pressure.

In fact, as we know, ARFID children don't respond to social pressures around eating, and because they are more anxious around meals, pressure to eat is even more unsuccessful and often causes a negative anxiety cycle to develop. Whenever such a cycle exists, it should be stopped. The best way to do this is to lower stress at mealtimes by using strategies such as distraction (see Chapter 10), to educate parents about ARFID (including explaining that it is not their fault) and to reassure them about the child's health, growth and nutrition.

Negative anxiety cycle

We know that ARFID is not the fault of parents. However, if undiagnosed and untreated, a negative anxiety cycle at mealtimes can develop. This usually begins with a sensory-sensitive and anxious avoidant child whose refusal of foods triggers the parent's worries about health, growth and nutrition, and perhaps associated feelings of blame and guilt. Due to these worries (which, remember, are very understandable), the parent becomes increasingly anxious and begins to use more forceful strategies at mealtimes. These strategies increase anxiety in the child which lowers appetite and increases their sensory sensitivity and vigilance to changes to their foods, resulting in further refusal. Unfortunately, this only serves to make the parent even more anxious and increases their desperation for the child to eat. This in turn increases the child's anxieties about foods and mealtimes, leading to more refusal, and so the cycle continues.

For some children, prompting, persuasion or encouragement at mealtimes may result in them eating too much. This particularly applies to autistic children who may have difficulties recognising feeling full. The result can be over-acceptance, overeating and obesity. Chapter 10 will cover ideas for managing this.

Hiding or disguising foods

This is a very common strategy and is usually done because of worries about growth and nutrition. It includes:

- hiding medicines or supplements

- hiding a 'healthy' food such as a vegetable in a preferred food

- adding extra calorie sources such as butter, milk or cream in a preferred food

- changing the appearance of a food to make it more likely to be eaten – for example, cutting foods into favourite shapes

- putting new foods into familiar packaging to 'trick' the child into accepting the new food.

Why don't these strategies work? As we have already seen in the first half of this book, this is because of the processes at work in ARFID – in particular, sensory hypersensitivity, neophobia, disgust and contamination responses. As a result, hiding a food, even one that we think is odourless, tasteless or so tiny that it is not visible, is likely to be spotted by the ARFID child.

> Toby's mum was worried about nutrition, and so she mixed an iron supplement into his favourite flavour of milkshake. Toby immediately spotted the change in taste and refused to accept that flavour of milkshake from Mum again.

> Masie's grandmother thought she could get Masie to eat more if she made a picture on the plate with her favourite foods. She cut up Masie's sausages into different shapes and made them into a smiley face. Unfortunately, Masie couldn't now recognise they were 'her' sausages and refused to eat them. When Masie's grandmother prepared them as usual the next time, Masie ate them as normal.

The same is true when the packaging of a food changes, where children with a visual hypersensitivity will spot the difference straight away. This is because the appearance of the packaging predicts the safety of the food inside.

> Liam eats the same brand of oven chips every day. His mother was very happy therefore when the price of his favourite chips was reduced. However, this changed when Liam saw the 'money off' change to the packaging and then refused to eat the chips.

Changes to packaging

As we have already seen, these children have difficulties filtering out relevant information which leads to a hypervigilance or over-checking that the food is okay and safe to eat. Any difference and the food is seen as not safe, the neophobic and disgust responses are triggered, and the food is rejected. We see this response particularly in autistic children who frequently appear to attend to the 'local' features of a food (the writing on the biscuit) rather than the 'global' or whole picture – that it is a familiar and liked biscuit.

Associated with sensory hypersensitivity and neophobia are disgust and contamination. This is where a new or disliked food that is mixed with or placed next to a familiar and liked food 'contaminates' the preferred food, leading to refusal of both foods. Unfortunately, it doesn't work the other way round: you can't get a child to like something new by putting it near the old food! If you are lucky, the child will only refuse the familiar food once, but if the contamination response is strong, you may lose it for good.

> Ellie's mother wanted her to eat peas and put a portion next to Ellie's favourite chicken nuggets. Ellie couldn't cope with them touching the chicken nuggets, and she refused to eat them until all the peas had been moved. Even then she had to scrape off the breaded part of the nuggets that had been touched by the peas, before she could eat the chicken.

Contamination fears are on a continuum, with some children having very extreme responses. For example, I know of one family where they keep the ARFID child's frozen potato products in a separate freezer from the frozen foods the rest of the family eat. This is because he will refuse his foods if the packets have touched other products he doesn't eat. Examples like this just serve to illustrate what families of ARFID children have to cope with and what the diagnosis calls 'marked interference with psychosocial functioning'. We will return to strategies for managing the impact of ARFID on families in later chapters.

Withholding preferred foods

Many families in clinic are worried about what their child is eating, particularly from a nutritional point of view. This is why they may withhold a preferred food or want their child to eat a 'healthier' food instead. Unfortunately, withholding a preferred food in favour of a healthier one is only likely to increase the child's anxiety and lead to refusal.

> Billy's parents wanted him to stop eating chocolate buttons and have a 'healthier' snack instead, so they gave him chocolate covered raisins. Billy took one look at the raisins and retched, saying they looked like 'rabbit poo'! Fortunately, he was still able to eat his chocolate buttons.

There are many messages in the media about 'healthy' eating or following a balanced diet with some foods (particularly those that are popular with ARFID children) labelled as 'junk'. Many of these messages are connected to the current rise in obesity and preventing children from becoming overweight. However, it should be remembered that the majority of children with ARFID are not at risk of becoming overweight. For them, foods that deliver a 'high calorie per mouthful' load are very beneficial, particularly if the child does not eat much in school (see Chapter 7). For these children, chocolate is a better calorie source than broccoli!

In addition, as we have already seen, the majority of children with ARFID do not appear to lack anything significant in their diet. This may be due to the fortification contained in some of the foods that are commonly eaten (see Chapter 6). For example, one of Rebecca's staple foods was a fortified breakfast cereal covered with melted chocolate. She ate this several times a day. She was fit and healthy and doing well at school. When she had a blood test, she was found to have normal levels of all major nutrients.

However, if you are a worried parent, ask your general practitioner, dietician or paediatrician to check for any nutritional deficiencies in your child. This generally involves a blood test, which is often difficult for a sensory-sensitive and anxious child to cope with. The ideas about managing anxiety in Chapters 10 and 11 may be able to help. These chapters also cover how to introduce a vitamin and mineral supplement to an ARFID child or teenager.

Rewards and bribery

If you are a parent of an ARFID child, you will already know that offering rewards or bribery does not work. Again, this is due to the processes that are underpinning ARFID and autism – in particular, high levels of disgust seen across children with ARFID (see Chapter 4) and some of the cognitive (thinking) differences seen in autism.

Reward or bribe?
Rewarding and bribing, although similar, are not the same. Rewards are earned for behaviour that is wanted – for example, eating a new and healthy food. Bribes are offered to avoid or stop something that isn't wanted – for example, eating a familiar and 'unhealthy' food. Regardless of the size of the incentive on offer, it is the intention behind the reward or bribe that is important. If it is planned and under the parent's control, it is most likely a reward; if it is done in desperation and negotiated by the child, it is most likely a bribe.

When we talk to groups of parents or professionals about ARFID, we always start by asking what foods they find disgusting. Some of the common responses are listed below. Without exception, when we suggest rewarding or bribing them to eat one of these foods, they always say no! This is because no reward or bribe is enough for them to overcome their disgust towards these foods. Our ARFID children are just the same, but even a different brand or flavour of a preferred food can be enough to trigger disgust.

Disgusting?

- Bananas – 'strong smell', 'too stringy'
- Mushrooms – 'too slimy', 'smells too earthy'
- Brussel sprouts – 'too bitter', 'was made to eat them at Christmas'
- Rice pudding – 'too lumpy', 'looks like vomit'
- Cheese – 'smells like feet', 'I don't want to eat mould'
- Squid – 'feels like rubber bands', 'smells too fishy'
- Liver – 'tastes of blood', 'I can't eat an organ!'

In addition to strong disgust responses, autistic children do not always respond to the promise of a reward or the threat of a punishment. For example, they might not understand that their computer time was stopped because they didn't stop playing their game when they were told to get ready for school. This does not mean they are being naughty or deliberately stubborn (even if that is how it feels!). It is rather that autistic children tend to be overly focused on details, such as the game, at the expense of understanding the overall meaning of a situation, such as the fact that it's time to go to school. This is known as weak central coherence and means that autistic people find it difficult to see the 'bigger picture' or connect fragmented details or events together.

Weak central coherence

Imagine walking into a new room. There are chairs and tables everywhere. Some people are sitting and eating and drinking or holding large pieces of cardboard. Other people are walking around and carrying plates, either empty or with food on them. There are a lot of different smells and noises.

Many of us would recognise this room as a restaurant. However, if you are autistic, this scene could be very confusing. You can't work out how the separate elements relate to each other – for example, that people carrying plates of food are taking them to the people sitting. Perhaps you are distracted by particular details, such as the pattern on the carpet. To you, these separate elements are fragmented and do not add up to the 'whole' of 'restaurant'.

There are some occasions where a reward (not a bribe) may be useful for a child with ARFID. For example, we have found that offering a reward after a child has tasted a new food for the first time can motivate them and help them overcome their anxiety. This is covered in more detail in Chapter 11.

Imitating others

Other people eating a food, or 'modelling', can help children eat a new and unfamiliar food. Imitating others eating is the process by which young children come out of the neophobic response and it naturally occurs at home and in other settings such as pre-school. As we have already seen, this carries a survival advantage in that children are then exposed to appropriate foods for their culture and they learn that these are okay and safe to eat (see Chapter 2).

However, we know that ARFID children, particularly those on the autism spectrum, do not imitate others eating in the same way and are not influenced by the social aspects of mealtimes. In fact, sitting an autistic ARFID child with others eating can end in disaster!

> When Amy started school, her teacher thought it would be a good idea for her to sit with her peers at lunch time, so that she could 'learn to eat what they were eating'. Amy was so disgusted by the foods the other children were having that she vomited and hid under the table.

As a result of these social differences, ARFID children can remain in the neophobic stage for a lot longer than their peers, perhaps even into adulthood. Some autistic children do mimic behaviour, including from favourite cartoon or TV characters. Mimicry tends to be less flexible and social than imitating and involves a direct copy of another's actions. However, this can also backfire.

> Michael has autism and a learning disability. He likes to watch a particular cartoon in which the main character frequently eats doughnuts. Michael would demand to eat similar doughnuts just like his favourite character as soon as the cartoon started – if these were not immediately available, Michael would become very distressed. Michael would only eat the doughnuts while watching the cartoon and never anywhere else.

Leaving the child to 'go hungry'

This is one of the most commonly used strategies by parents and one that is often advised by professionals. The rationale is that if left for a period of time, the child will become hungry and naturally and spontaneously want to eat. However, for ARFID children this strategy fundamentally misunderstands what is going on.

One of the diagnostic criteria for ARFID (DSM-5; APA 2013) is that the child has little interest in eating. For many, this means a lack of recognition and expression of hunger. Parents often report that their child never comments or behaves as if they are hungry, by asking for food or rummaging in the fridge. A lack of recognition of hunger may also be part of an interoceptive response. This is where awareness of internal bodily states such as hunger, pain, temperature and mood are often poor.

These differences are particularly reported in autistic individuals. Whatever the reason, leaving a child with ARFID to 'go hungry' carries serious risks.

> When Zoe's parents were advised not to offer her preferred snacks during the day but only to offer 'healthy' meals, Zoe refused to eat anything. Her family thought that after a day or so she would get hungry and accept the meals. However, Zoe did not eat or drink for several days and was subsequently admitted to hospital with dehydration and weight loss.

It cannot be stressed enough that this is a potentially dangerous strategy and one that can have serious consequences. We will deal with how to manage a child with problems recognising and responding to appetite in the following chapters. For now, if anyone recommends that you leave a child with ARFID to go hungry, ignore them!

Summary

- Almost anything can stop a child with ARFID from eating.
- Knowing what *not* to do, and why, is as important as knowing what to do.
- Pressuring children leads to anxiety and more refusal. This is particularly true when a negative anxiety cycle develops at mealtimes.
- Hiding and disguising foods or medicines can contaminate the food they are hidden in and can lead to that food being lost from the diet.
- Withholding preferred foods in favour of healthier ones leads to refusal and potentially to weight loss.
- Using rewards or bribes does not overcome the food refusal seen in ARFID and autism.

- Children with ARFID do not imitate other people eating and remain 'stuck' in the neophobic response for longer than other children.

- Leaving an ARFID child to go long periods of time without eating or drinking can be dangerous and lead to dehydration, weight loss and health issues.

. . .

Tips for parents and carers

- Don't pressurise the child to eat.
- Don't hide or disguise foods or medicine in other foods.
- Don't withhold preferred foods in favour of healthy foods.
- Don't use rewards or bribes.
- Don't expect the child to imitate others eating.
- Don't leave the child to go hungry.
- Seek professional support to help stop negative anxiety cycles at mealtimes.

. . .

Chapter 10

Interventions with the Younger Child

Where have we got to?

In the previous chapter we discussed what doesn't work and why. Now we will move on to what does work and a range of evidence-based interventions. This chapter will cover what is appropriate for younger children up to the age of eight or so, and for those with developmental delay and/or learning disabilities. Chapter 11 will cover what is appropriate for older children and teenagers who have fewer learning or developmental needs.

> **What do we mean by 'evidence-based'?**
> Parents reading this book may not be familiar with the expression 'evidence-based practice'. This term generally refers to the combination of research evidence, clinical expertise and patient values. As a result, much of this book is underpinned by academic theory and research in the field of feeding and eating behaviour. However, as the famous physicist Albert Einstein (also now thought to have had Asperger's syndrome!) said: 'Not everything that can be counted counts, and not everything that counts can be counted.' That is why *practice*-based evidence is also important. For this book, and particularly for this section on interventions, we have also relied on our own clinical experience and the experience of families as a source of what might work with children with ARFID.

Before you begin

Before you begin any intervention, it is worth stopping and asking what you are trying to aim for. Ask yourself the following questions:

- Am I aiming to increase the *amount* of food eaten?
- Am I aiming to increase the *range* of foods eaten?

These aims, although related, are not the same. For children who are underweight and failing to grow according to their growth pattern (called 'growth faltering'), the most important thing is to increase the amount of calories consumed. Maintaining weight and growth have priority over increasing the range of foods. For children who are growing as expected, increasing the amount of calories consumed is not necessary, and in fact could lead to weight gain. For these children, introducing different foods to expand their range would be the aim.

It is also important to consider not just *what* to do, but *when*. We have found using a stepped approach is the most effective way of achieving goals and not overloading the child or family with too much to do at once. This is particularly important for autistic children who may have multiple difficulties and require interventions and supports for other issues as well as eating. In addition, not every intervention idea will be appropriate for every child, so consider them as a 'tool-box' to choose from depending on each child's individual circumstances. The following strategies are listed in the order we usually suggest them to families in clinic, and, as such, they build on each other.

Remember, we are writing a new rule book. It doesn't matter that your child doesn't sit at a table with the rest of the family, that they don't use a knife and fork, that they don't eat the same foods as everyone else. What does matter is they are getting enough calories and that they (and everyone else in the family) are happy at meal and snack times.

Managing autism

For an autistic child, it is essential that their autism is managed as well as possible before making any changes to their eating. The following are some general strategies:

- Keep routines stable at home and at school. This will reduce anxiety.

- Use timetables or schedules. These help the child predict what is happening next.

- Use visual aids to help the child cope with their environment.

- Use sensory interventions. These help the child feel settled.

- Avoid stressful periods when making any changes – for example, Christmas is not a good time to introduce a new food!

Managing growth, health and nutrition

As we have already seen, the majority of children with ARFID maintain their growth pattern if they are allowed their preferred and safe foods. This is because they are able to regulate their growth from the calories in these foods. In fact, most families we see in clinic have already worked out that if they allow the preferred foods, the child grows well.

If a child is losing weight, or not growing as expected, it is important to look for reasons why. Frequently, foods are further restricted by the child during a period of stress. For example, we get many families contacting us in September at the start of the new school year and around Christmas when routines change. Reducing the stress, if possible, or minimising its impact is crucial. During these times only offer the most preferred foods and stick to 'high calorie per mouthful' foods or add in extra snacks, again with preferred and calorie-dense foods.

For parents who are concerned about nutrition, a vitamin and mineral supplement can be useful. However, this is not an easy thing to get an ARFID child to accept! The same is true of medicines, and the following ideas apply to both:

- Choose a supplement that has a similar flavour, texture or colour to the child's preferences around foods.

- Be prepared to experiment; it might take several attempts to get it right.

- Involve more able children in choosing a supplement themselves.

- Try the supplement in the same staged way as trying a new food (see Chapter 11).

- Have a 'rule' about taking it and offer a reward immediately afterwards.

- Allow a preferred drink or food immediately after having the supplement.

- Do not hide a supplement in a food. The sensory-sensitive child will spot and reject it!

- Use a syringe to give medicines if necessary.

- Distract the child to lower anxiety (see below).

Amy's mother was worried about nutrition, particularly when Amy stopped eating a breakfast cereal. She introduced a supplement by choosing one with a flavour Amy liked (strawberry) and a texture she could cope with (melt in the mouth). It also helped that the supplement was pink; this was the colour of Amy's favourite cartoon character.

Managing appetite

As we have already seen, ARFID children have difficulties recognising and responding to appetite and hunger cues. The same can also be true for feelings of being full, or 'satiety', particularly when the child is on the autism spectrum. Managing the barriers to recognising and responding to hunger is important early on in an intervention programme.

Many children with ARFID 'graze' rather than eat meals, so scheduling regular meal and snack times is a good way to help them begin to regulate appetite and respond accordingly. Scheduling works to ensure that the child is having a regular calorie intake which maintains energy levels. It also helps 'cue' in the connection between 'it is time to eat' and associated bodily feelings of hunger and appetite. We recommend six scheduled daily eating 'opportunities' (e.g. three meals and three snacks). This is because intake in ARFID is better with short, frequent meal opportunities.

Setting a daily eating schedule

- Include eating opportunities in daily routines at home and school.
- Use visual aids for non-verbal children.
- Adapt the schedule to accommodate individual family routines.
- Each eating opportunity should last no more than around 20–30 minutes.
- Do not allow the child to go more than three hours without eating, for example:
  - 08.00 breakfast
  - 10.30 snack at school
  - 13.00 lunch
  - 15.30 snack after school
  - 18.00 dinner
  - 20.30 snack before bed.

Scheduling also helps children who show 'compensation' and eat a lot in one sitting, such as after school. As we have seen in Chapter 5, this is not the same as 'binge eating', where large amounts of food are eaten very quickly, almost as if the person is out of control. This is a serious mental health issue and is very different from compensation where a child is simply making up for missing calories. Children who compensate are often doing so because their preferred foods were not available to them earlier, or they were too anxious or engrossed in a favourite activity to eat. For these children, interventions that manage anxiety (see below) are recommended.

Another major barrier to managing appetite is constipation which can cause a reduction in appetite and how much the child eats. Seek a referral to a paediatrician or gastroenterologist if your child has infrequent bowel movements; they should prescribe medication to help. Ideas for helping an ARFID child take medication are listed above.

Overeating

Occasionally we see children in clinic who do not respond to signs that they are full. These children, who are often on the autism spectrum, may eat too much and be at risk of weight gain and obesity. For a child who overeats, we may have to control portion size, or use a plate guard to measure out portions. It may also be necessary to restrict access to high-calorie foods or swap these for lower-calorie versions. For these children, increasing physical activity can be an easier intervention than getting them to eat 'healthier' foods. Good exercises include walking, swimming and the trampoline.

Managing sensory issues

Children with ARFID are likely to be sensory over-responsive or 'hypersensitive'. This has an impact on what foods they can accept and their behaviours around mealtimes. Children who are hypersensitive are more likely to:

- refuse foods
- refuse preferred foods if the appearance of food/ packaging changes

- dislike getting their hands and face messy
- refuse foods with lumps or texture, or foods mixed together
- experience sensory 'overload' at mealtimes and become overwhelmed and anxious.

Sensory overload

Many ARFID children easily experience sensory 'overload'. Put simply, it is when the sensory channels receive too much information at once, and the child cannot filter out what is important and what does not need attending to. It is like having too many programmes open on a computer: everything starts to slow down and eventually the system crashes. For children, it leads to confusion, frustration, anxiety and, frequently, meltdowns. Adapting the environment can help the overloaded child. This makes it easier for them to manage their behaviour and anxiety so that they can focus on eating. The following are some ideas:

- Allow the child to eat in an environment with few visual distractions.
- Allow the child to eat away from others such as a bedroom or classroom.
- Provide a sensory safe eating space/den – for example, a play tent.

Specifically for autistic children:

- Encourage the child to wear ear defenders to minimise noise.
- Block out extra visual information using sunglasses and/or a hat/hoodie.

Desensitisation

Children with hypersensitivity will try to block out the sensations that are uncomfortable, often by avoiding the sensation altogether or by going into 'shutdown' or 'meltdown'. In addition to adaptations in the environment, desensitisation helps the child to learn to tolerate a greater range of sensations such as different tastes, textures and smells. This is done through a gradual and controlled exposure to a disliked sensation. It is suitable for use across the age range and spectrum of ability, and we will return to it in Chapter 11 to show how it can be used for older children and teenagers.

A desensitisation programme involves recognising what is difficult for the child, introducing gradual steps to increase tolerance and a careful monitoring of the child's responses. Such programmes are often developed by health professionals, such as speech and language or occupational therapists. However, there are things that parents can do at home once they understand some general principles:

- Little and often is best. Five minutes once or twice a day is better than half an hour every week.

- Firm touch is easier to tolerate than gentle touch. Think about being stroked by a feather. It can be ticklish and uncomfortable.

- Work from parts of the body where touch is easier for the child to accept, towards those where it is more difficult.

- If the child becomes upset, it is a sign that you are going too quickly. Slow down and go back a stage.

- Watch the child's responses carefully to avoid upsetting them. Always end a desensitisation activity on a good note.

We recommend beginning with the child's hands, moving on to the face and lips, and eventually inside the mouth. This is where touch is likely to be hardest for the sensory-sensitive ARFID child. The following are some ideas for each of these areas:

- Desensitising hands:
  - Encourage finger painting and handprints.
  - Massage the child using slow, smooth movements on parts of their body that they will accept. Gradually,

move towards the hands from other areas of the body – for example, upper arm to lower arm to wrist to back of hand and palm and fingers. This is an ideal activity to do while the child is having a bath, with a sponge and bath cream.

- ◦ Encourage the child to play with sand, modelling or cooking dough or other textures which can be modelled, squashed, rolled or shaped.

- ◦ Encourage 'messy play' (see below). Start with drier textures and work up to sticky textures, as these are harder to cope with.

• Desensitising face and lips:

- ◦ Encourage finger and mouth play – blow raspberries, make kissing noises, or sing 'Pat-a-cake' while patting the cheeks.

- ◦ Encourage blowing through straws or whistles.

- ◦ Use stroking and patting movements on the child's head and face. You can stroke the whole face and gradually work towards the mouth – for example, top of head to outer edge of face to central area of face to lips and inside of mouth. Use different materials to do this.

- ◦ Let the child play with face creams and make-up to allow a gradual touch to the face.

- ◦ Encourage face painting. Start at the hairline and work towards the mouth.

- ◦ Make lip prints. Use lipstick to start with and then progress to food such as chocolate spread, honey or jam.

• Desensitising inside the mouth:

- ◦ Encourage the child to bring foods and suitable objects to their mouth and to lick, suck and taste them. Use mouthing toys for very young children and for older children a 'chew-buddy' (a specially designed oral-motor chewing toy).

- Encourage the child to touch these objects and foods to the insides of their mouth and explore them with their tongue. This will help the tongue get used to feeling different textures and develop a wider range of movement.

- Rub a finger or a toothbrush along the child's upper and lower gums. Rub on the outside first, then on the inside of the gums.

- Get the child to look in a mirror and touch their teeth with their fingers all the way round to the back of the mouth. They can copy an adult doing this first.

- It may then be possible to introduce a little toothpaste or a taste of a food.

- When introducing a new food, give regular exposure to the same foods over time. This will help the child know what the foods feel like and how to manage them in the mouth.

For ARFID children, particularly where they are stuck on liquid or pureed diets, the sides of the mouth may be very sensitive, making teeth brushing and chewing foods difficult. These children usually require a specific programme written by an appropriate health professional, such as a speech and language therapist. The aim is for the child to be able to explore foods that they can hold, take to the mouth and move around the mouth, particularly to the sides of the mouth and lips where the sensitivity is likely to be the most extreme.

Messy play

Messy play helps a child tolerate touching different textures and foods. The earlier and more frequently a child is exposed the better. For parents who find mess difficult to tolerate, preparation can help, such as covering the floor or the table with a groundsheet or rubber mat to make it easier to clean up afterwards. Wherever possible, resist the urge to get the wipes out. Messy play is also an ideal activity for nursery and school.

It is also important to be clear about what you are trying to achieve – that is, exposing the child to a range of sensory experiences to help build up a tolerance; it is not necessarily aimed at eating. That is why it is a good idea to keep foods that are being tasted separate from the textures being used in messy play. Making potato prints is fun, but it doesn't generally result in the child wanting to eat potatoes! Always start with drier textures such as dry pasta, rice, lentils, string and beads, and work up to the stickier and wetter ones – cooked pasta, foam, wet sand, wet paint, yoghurt – as these are harder for the sensory-hypersensitive child to cope with.

For slightly older children, games are a good way of desensitising. The beauty of a game is that it distracts the child from any discomfort, meaning they are less anxious and will notice any uncomfortable feelings less and be more motivated to take part. I have yet to meet an ARFID child who does not like to win!

Sticky fingers game
- Choose a food that comes in small-size portions and which starts to melt at body temperature – for example, chocolate buttons/balls.
- Divide these into two piles, one for you and one for the child.
- Have two jars, one for you and one for the child.
- Now race the child to see who can get their pile in the jar first by picking up the chocolate one piece at a time.
- The child will be so busy trying to win they won't notice how sticky their fingers have become!

Many ARFID children, particularly those on the autism spectrum, benefit from assessment and input from specialist health professionals for their sensory issues. This can highlight the individual 'sensory profile' of a child and lead to a sensory 'diet'. This is an intervention plan, specific to that child, which includes all their sensory needs, not just those around food. See Table 7.1 for details of which professionals can help with sensory issues.

Managing rigidity

One of the core features of ARFID is the rigidity seen in food choices. As we have already seen, many ARFID children stick to very particular examples of foods, are extremely brand-loyal and only accept foods in familiar packaging. These choices represent learned safety: the child knows that this is their usual food and is therefore safe to eat. Autistic children are also likely to display additional rigidity in what is known as the 'desire for sameness'. This manifests itself in an adherence to routines and rituals around foods and mealtimes, and is related to difficulties predicting the world.

The ability to make category generalisations, or understand the concepts that link foods together, helps us predict a food – for example, understanding that a previously unknown biscuit is likely to be brown, sweet and crunchy and similar to other biscuits we have eaten and enjoyed. This ability to generalise across different examples of foods appears to be lacking in ARFID where each new biscuit, or one that looks different from the norm, is treated with suspicion and rejected despite the fact that the child loves biscuits. This presents a major problem to families where the rigid adherence to very few specific examples of foods causes difficulties when those foods can't be found.

Spreading the sets

Expanding the safe categories of foods the child already accepts helps build these generalisation skills. We call this 'spreading the sets' and it is done gradually, one food at a time. It works best where the child is not too anxious about intake and starts with the most familiar and accepted categories of foods first. Spreading the sets involves the following steps:

1. Look for similarities in the foods the child accepts. Is there a 'bread', 'crisp' or 'biscuit' category, for example?

2. Pick a category of foods that look similar to each other, such as bread, biscuits, crisps.

3. Offer a slight variation of a food within that category – for example, unsliced bread instead of sliced bread or a new brand or flavour of the same crisp.

4. Only make one change at a time. Don't pick a new brand and flavour at the same time.

5. Offer the new food in small tastes and away from mealtimes (see 'Taste trials' in Chapter 11).

6. Use distraction, relaxation and new contexts (see below) to support the child in trying the different food.

Figure 10.1 gives some ideas of how to do this with crisps. For example, you might start by choosing another brand of crisp, which looks similar (and is a similar flavour) to the one your child already accepts. Or you might choose a different shape of crisp from the child's preferred brand, or one that is exactly the same brand and type of crisp but a different flavour. The key is to only change one thing (brand/shape/flavour) at a time.

'Spreading the sets' with crisps

Sometimes parents question this strategy, particularly the wisdom of adding another, similar type of food into the diet. This is understandable and usually occurs when the parent doesn't want their child to eat any more 'unhealthy' foods such as crisps. In fact, some parents are so worried about this that they do not even admit these are favourite foods for their child! However, there are a number of advantages. It combats 'sensory-specific satiety', which is where foods are dropped from the diet due to the brain signalling a lack of variety. Adding a similar version of a food to the child's diet means that there is always another example of that food, meaning if a food is dropped it is not completely lost. It also gives families more choice, particularly when away from home, and reduces the worries about getting hold of the preferred foods. We have also found that over time spreading the sets helps the child to be more flexible and able to accept bigger changes to their diet. This is particularly important for those children who lack confidence; making one small change increases their belief that they will be able to continue making other, bigger changes.

Another related strategy is to help the child understand how foods are similar using the 'same as' analogy. Figure 10.2 gives the example of how you might help the child to understand that the potato inside a baked potato is the 'same as' (or similar to) mashed potato. Once again, this is best done visually, either using pictures or real foods and involving the child as much as possible in the preparation of these.

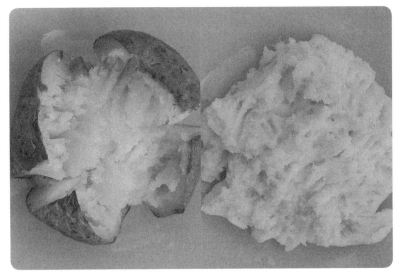

'Same as'

Managing anxiety

Anxiety, either directly related to foods, or in general, has a very negative impact on eating. As we have already seen, the 'fight or flight' response shuts off our digestive system, making it extremely difficult to eat when we are stressed. Anxiety directly affects eating by decreasing appetite, increasing sensory sensitivity and vigilance to changes in foods, and increasing refusal of foods, even preferred ones. Extra anxiety in families, particularly around mealtimes, also increases a child's refusal. In addition, autistic children also frequently have additional anxieties due to their social, emotional and cognitive differences – for example, in understanding and predicting the world around them, which is one of the reasons autistic children often find change very hard. Reducing anxiety, including general anxiety, therefore has many benefits when it comes to eating.

Anxiety may manifest in a variety of ways depending on the child's age and learning needs. For younger children and those with a learning disability or who are non-verbal, the signs may be in physical symptoms and/or in behaviour – for example:

- agitation
- weight loss
- stomach pain or headaches, dizziness, tremors
- increase in challenging or self-injurious behaviours
- difficulties sleeping
- difficulties going to the toilet or going frequently
- becoming more obsessive
- stronger than usual fixation on routines.

Young children and those with learning disabilities are not yet able to use their thinking skills to help them deal with anxiety. As a result, strategies such as relaxation that address the physical symptoms of anxiety, or those that involve environmental adaptations such as reducing sensory overload, are likely to be the most successful. To anticipate when anxiety might happen, it can help to keep a record of previous episodes and always have an emergency strategy for calming a child down. This might include, for example, moving them to a calm and quite environment. If you are a parent and continue to be a concerned about your child's levels of anxiety, seek additional support from appropriate health professionals, such as your GP or Child and Adolescent Mental Health Services (CAMHS).

Relaxation activities

- Teach the child to breathe deeply using bubbles. This calms the body down quickly. Challenge them to blow the biggest bubble, which can only be done by breathing in and out slowly.
- Make a collage of calming and relaxing pictures that the child can look at.
- Teach muscle relaxation by pretending to be a wobbly jelly or a rag doll. Wobbling or loosening the body gets rid of tension.
- Write a story about a calm and relaxing space or use a story from a website or app (there are many resources available for free).
- Get support for relaxation – for example, a child-friendly yoga class.
- Encourage exercise such as walking, swimming, trampoline.
- Use sensory soothing and calming activities – for example, listening to music, having a bath, sensory toys/objects.
- It can be a good idea to offer a new or different food after a relaxation activity.

For most families there are times in the year where due to changes to routines, such as transitions, school holidays or Christmas, anxiety is ever-present and is difficult to change. The following are recommended to support the maximum intake of the child's preferred foods during any extended period of anxiety:

- Offer only preferred foods. A period of stress is not the time to try a new food.
- Offer more foods at snack times; these tend to be less pressured than mealtimes.
- Use distraction while eating, such as watching a favourite TV programme.

Using distraction

When I watch a film in the cinema, it always surprises me that the popcorn disappears so quickly! Most of us will eat more when distracted by an enjoyable activity, and this can be used as an intervention:

- Pair a meal/snack with a favourite activity such as a TV programme/DVD.
- Allow the child to engage in the activity while eating.
- End the activity when the child stops eating, even if the child hasn't finished the food.
- Repeat this at the same meal/snack time each day. This teaches the child that the mealtime and the activity go together, and that as long as they carry on eating, the activity will continue.
- Pair a specific food with a particular activity. This can work well if trying to introduce something new.
- For slow eaters choose a programme that is relatively short (15–20 minutes) and tell the child that the food has to be finished by the time the programme ends. This is a good strategy for breakfast, where time can be short! A visual timer such as an egg timer can help a child understand how much time they have left.

Managing routines and rituals

Children with ARFID, particularly those on the autism spectrum, can have fixed routines and rituals around food and mealtimes. These often include:

- having to sit in the same seat at mealtimes
- foods having to be prepared by the same person
- eating a specific number of foods
- eating foods in a particular order

- foods having to be arranged in exactly the same way on the plate
- only using specific utensils.

These routines and rituals are likely to be connected to the learned safety response in ARFID and the additional anxiety caused by living in an unpredictable world for those on the autistic spectrum. They can be difficult to change. However, it helps to try to understand the reasons behind a routine or ritual. Complex rituals, such as those seen in autistic children, appear to help the child have some control over their environment. Keeping as much variety and spontaneity in family life as possible can prevent rituals from becoming too restricted in the first place.

> Tom, aged 11, is autistic and non-verbal. He only drinks a particular formula milk from a baby's bottle. The bottle has to be exactly the same one, as does the teat (he can tell if it has been washed or changed), and only his mum can prepare the bottle. He will only drink in the lounge while watching a particular cartoon.

For some children, particularly those on the autism spectrum, fixed routines can be an advantage, especially where there is a new context coming up. Do you remember my young man from the introduction to this book who would only eat spaghetti hoops on toast? This was a new food he accepted within the new context of being in the residential school and which he then ate every other day he spent there, but he never ate it away from this context. We are not sure exactly why this behaviour develops, but it appears the food and the context become connected and stored almost as one 'category', with the context also predicting the safety of the food.

So how do we use this behaviour to introduce a new food? All new contexts, such as a new school, respite, play scheme or youth club, represent a good opportunity to introduce a new food. This should be done by offering the new food the very first time the child goes there – for example, by sending the food to the new context or organising in advance for the food to be available and offered to the child. It is also possible to add in a new routine into a familiar context and in a similar way offer new food at the same time. For example, by going home a different way from school and stopping at a new café en route. In addition, sometimes a child will try something new within both familiar and unfamiliar contexts for a preferred teacher.

New context, new food

- Choose a context away from home. Routines at home are generally more fixed and harder to adapt than those in different locations.

- Maximise opportunities where there is a large change in context – for example, the child going to a new school. These appear to be more successful than smaller changes such as going up to a new class.

- Offer a new food in the new context as soon as the child goes there – for example, the first night of youth club.

- Use a preferred adult, if possible, within the new context to offer the new food.

- Adapt established routines to allow a new activity and food – for example, going to the park on the way home from school and offering a new snack food there.

- Establish a new regular activity and offer a new food as part of the routine of the activity – for example, going swimming and having a 'swimming food' in the café afterwards.

Remember with these strategies that the food is likely to stay entirely within that context or routine and is not usually eaten elsewhere. It is important that parents understand that the food may never cross into another context, including home. However, this does not mean the parent is doing something wrong – quite the opposite. In fact, these strategies have the advantage of increasing the range of foods the child eats across their whole day or week and taking the pressure off parents to be expanding the child's range of foods at home.

Summary

- It is important to establish the aims of an intervention before beginning.

- Maintaining weight always has priority over increasing dietary range.

- Allowing preferred foods maintains growth, health and nutrition, particularly in times of stress.

- Scheduling regular eating opportunities helps the child with ARFID to recognise and respond to hunger cues and improves intake.

- Managing sensory overload can help the child eat more and cope at mealtimes.

- Using desensitisation helps a child with sensory hypersensitivity to tolerate and cope around foods. Messy play is a great way to do this as it is fun and enjoyable.

- Anxiety in ARFID increases sensory hypersensitivity, vigilance to foods and refusal. Interventions that reduce both general and food-specific anxiety can increase intake and range.

- ARFID/autistic children can be rigid and stick to very specific examples of foods in narrow categories. Expanding these categories can widen the child's range and give more choice.

- Children with ARFID, particularly those on the autism spectrum, often eat particular foods in specific contexts.

- New contexts can be a good time to offer a new food.

- Routines and rituals can be adapted, or added to, in order to introduce new foods.

. . .

Tips for parents and carers

- Always allow your child's preferred foods, and in times of stress offer only these.

- Add a vitamin and mineral supplement to your child's diet, if needed and where possible.

- Schedule regular eating opportunities. This helps your child learn to recognise being hungry.

- Desensitise your child and manage sensory overload. This reduces anxiety around foods and increases your child's ability to tolerate and cope with different sensory experiences.

- Watch for signs that your child is anxious. If you are concerned, seek a referral to an appropriate health professional.

- Use relaxation and distraction to reduce your child's anxiety, particularly around mealtimes.

- Keep as much variety and spontaneity in family life as possible. This will reduce the development and impact of rituals and routine.

- Introduce new foods to your child that are very similar to already accepted ones.

- Use any new context or routine as an opportunity to add a new food to your child's diet.

. . .

Chapter 11

Interventions with the Older Child

Where have we got to?

In the previous chapter we looked at interventions with the younger child and for those with developmental delay and/ or learning disabilities. This chapter will cover what works for older children (aged 8 and above) and teenagers who have fewer learning or developmental needs.

Much of this chapter will be on managing the anxiety associated with food in ARFID. It will also cover how to try new foods and becoming more independent around mealtimes. For older children and for teenagers, motivation is the key to them being able to move on; once they gain some incentive for making changes to their eating, many other interventions become possible, not least for managing anxiety. Chapter 8 discusses the importance of motivation, including the signs when a young person might be ready to move on.

Not all of the ideas listed below will be applicable to all older children or teenagers. Rather, they should be considered as part of a 'tool-kit' that young people themselves can take ownership of and use when they feel ready. We have also found a stepped approach, using one intervention at a time and building on the successes at each stage, to be very useful for the older age group – in particular, when it comes to dealing with eating issues alongside other, problematic aspects of growing older, especially in the teenage years.

Autism and the teenage years

As young people develop, so does their autism, and the teenage years can be particularly challenging. For some young people, the autism diagnosis comes in adolescence and after long-standing issues with food. Although recognition of the difficulties is positive, sometimes the adjustment to the new autism label can cause additional anxiety and further restriction in eating. For some, this also becomes an issue of control, and weight loss can occur. As a result, these young people are likely to need continuing support through their teenage years to understand what autism means for them and to manage their anxiety, particularly to prevent further restriction of foods.

Managing growth, health and nutrition

Just as it is for younger children, allowing preferred foods is the number-one intervention for older ARFID children and teenagers. This maintains growth, health and nutrition and is particularly important during periods of stress such as exam time, or, for those on the autism spectrum, periods of transition such as moving schools.

If you are a parent and you want to make sure your child or teenager is getting the right nutrition, introducing a vitamin and mineral supplement is a good idea. You can do this by consulting a dietician who can advise on what might be the right one for your child. For this age group, learning how to take a supplement or medicine is an important life skill and one that is worth spending some time to master. Chapter 10 gives some ideas about how to choose and introduce a supplement or medicine. In addition, this older age group can be more involved in choosing a supplement and this can be similar to the process of choosing a new food to try (see the section below on 'Taste trials' for ideas).

Tom is 14 and has ARFID. Tom's psychologist taught him to take a supplement by using the 'same as' strategy. They picked a supplement that was the same shape and colour as a favourite sweet. Tom then desensitised to the feel of this in his mouth by cutting it up into pieces and learning to tolerate the feel using slightly larger pieces each time. Eventually, Tom was able to take the whole supplement.

Managing appetite

Older children and teenagers also have difficulties recognising and managing appetite. In fact, the ARFID criterion of 'apparent lack of interest in eating or food' is often very obvious in this age group. I've lost count of the number of young people with ARFID who've told me that if I could invent a pill which meant they would never have to eat again they'd take it! It is also common in this age group to show compensation, or eating a lot of the preferred foods in one sitting. This is usually because these foods are not available at a mealtime, such as at school or college, or because anxiety or being engrossed in a favourite activity means the young person does not register and respond to the bodily signs of it being 'time to eat'.

Compensating can be extreme. For example, Will discovered a liking for frankfurter sausages and ate 300 of these over one weekend! This added up to approximately 12,000Kcals; however, during the previous week he had eaten very little. So all Will was really doing that weekend was making up for the calorie load that he had missed. However, it is a good idea to help young people learn to recognise and respond to appetite cues in order for them to eat more regularly. I have found 'mindfulness' techniques to be useful tools for helping young people with ARFID begin to notice whereabouts in their body they feel hunger.

Mindfulness for appetite

Mindfulness is a technique developed from Eastern meditation practice and is used as a relaxation and stress relief technique. Mindfulness involves paying attention (e.g. to oneself, the environment) in the present moment and without judgement. There are many standard mindfulness exercises, but the most useful for appetite is the 'body scan'. This is where each part of the body is paid attention to, or 'scanned', in order to notice any feelings present there, such as tension, pain or relaxation. I have found the following exercise, which only takes a few minutes, to be useful for helping an older child or teenager notice the signs of hunger. It is best done just before a usual meal or snack time.

- Sitting or lying down, imagine a scanner passing over your body.

- At each point in your body (feet, legs, pelvis, stomach, chest, arms, head) try to notice any feelings present there. Where and what are they?

- Now hover the scanner above your stomach. What feelings are present there? Can you notice hunger? What does this feel like? Describe the feeling in as much detail as possible.

I have found that older children or teenagers, particularly if independent in their eating at school or college, often skip breakfast or lunch, usually due to anxiety about the day, a lack of available foods and/or embarrassment about their eating. It is therefore important to schedule regular eating opportunities; Chapter 10 gives a suggested daily eating schedule. Older children and young people can take more responsibility by setting reminders to eat on a mobile phone or carrying portable preferred foods with them to school, college or any other regular activity away from home. Parents may also need to help to negotiate that these foods are allowed in these environments.

Managing rigidity

As we saw in Chapter 10, rigidity is a core feature of ARFID and can lead to a learned safety in the way foods are chosen, prepared, presented and eaten. For autistic children, rigidity is also a core issue and results in a 'desire for sameness' with routines and rituals developing around foods and mealtimes. For some young people, this rigidity provides a coping mechanism for dealing with stress; for others, especially those who are motivated, rigidity can be an advantage in helping them move on.

> Rosie prepares her own food which involves a long and elaborate ritual that includes using exactly the same utensils, arranging foods in order on her plate and watching the same TV programme at mealtimes. Rosie explained that the ritual helps her cope with the stress of school.

> Robert has Asperger's syndrome and is very literal. He wants to make some changes to his eating, having become interested in nutrition at school. We devised some food 'rules', such as eating a certain number of calories every day from a selection of food groups. Robert has made a spreadsheet and planned his meals so that he can stick to the rules.

During periods of stress, routines and rituals often increase in frequency and intensity. If the routine or ritual is manageable and does not cause any additional stress to other family members, then it may be possible to let the young person continue with it. However, if it is causing them distress, or if it is becoming impossible to manage family life, then it might be time to intervene. Finding alternative ways to manage anxiety is therefore important. If you decide to use rules around foods, it is important that these are meaningful to the young person and that they are in control of them in order for them to work. Harnessing technology can help and it can be a structured way of them becoming more independent around eating.

Managing sensory issues

In the older age group with ARFID we see similar sensory hypersensitivities in relation to foods as we do with younger children. Using desensitisation and managing sensory overload are also good strategies, particularly if these are adapted to be age-appropriate.

Teen 'overload'

Older children and teenagers, even those on the autism spectrum, can be acutely aware of any differences between them and their peer group. As a result, helping them cope in overloading environments works best if the strategies are discreet and easily managed by the young person themselves. The following are some examples suitable for school and other public environments:

- Negotiate a 'pass-out' at school to be used when the classroom becomes too much – for example, being sent on an errand by the teacher.
- Locate a sensory safe space in school/college such as the library.
- Use relaxation to lower anxiety – for example, deep breathing.
- Get support from a trusted teacher or friend.

For autistic young people:

- Replace ear defenders with small (and less noticeable) earphones or foam ear plugs.
- Cut out unwanted visual stimuli with a hat, hoodie or dark glasses.

Desensitisation

Desensitisation is a very useful and often very effective strategy with the older age group. We use it in two main ways. The first is to encourage the young person to spend as much time as they can around foods and people eating. This might involve, for example, helping prepare or cook foods, sitting with friends eating or deliberately visiting a café or restaurant. At this stage, the goal is not necessarily to eat something new but to gradually get used to the sights, smells and textures of different foods and tolerating other people eating next to them. In order to do this, the young person has to overcome their initial anxieties (which is why being motivated is necessary) and work out their own sensory tolerance levels. The goal here is to be able to challenge themselves and move out of their 'comfort zone', but not to the extent that it is overloading or distressing. Sometimes it happens very naturally and due to circumstances.

> Dan has a new puppy, and it is his responsibility to look after her including giving her food and cleaning up after she has pooed. Initially, Dan found this extremely difficult and couldn't cope with the sights and smells, and Mum had to do these jobs. Over time, as Dan has 'desensitised', he doesn't notice the smells so much and is able to do these jobs himself.

The second way in which we use desensitisation is in relation to a specific food. This usually happens as part of a 'taste trial' (see below), where the young person has chosen the food themselves and is considering trying it. In this age group, we often find that the young person is often very visually hypersensitive and will often reject a food on sight, particularly where the appearance (including the packaging) has changed. This varies in severity, and a good way to test how visually sensitive a young person is, is to see if they can distinguish between two brands of a similar food on sight without the packaging.

For these visually sensitive young people, the process of choosing a new food to try involves a gradual 'visual desensitisation', as they slowly get used to the way the new food looks. This can be done in a deliberate and staged way, and is the first step in an overall desensitisation programme to that new food. The following steps can be done with a young person:

1. Identify a possible new food – for example, chips.

2. Look at examples of chips, via an internet search engine or pictures in magazines.

3. Ask the young person questions such as what brand or type (e.g. frozen/chip shop/fries) and how they should be cooked. The goal is for them to explain what the food should ideally look like in order for them to be able to taste it.

4. Make a collage of examples that the young person decides they might be able to try.

5. Challenge the young person to go and look at these in real life in a café or restaurant or to watch someone else eat them.

6. At this stage the challenge is just to look not to taste!

The image below gives an example of a collage of chips. Looking at the different types of chip, for example, can help the young person choose the one that looks most 'right' for them. Following this they can then begin to desensitise to the other sensory properties of the food.

Visual desensitisation with chips

Once the young person has become desensitised to the look of a food, they then need to learn to tolerate the feel and the texture. This is best done using the specific food in question, and literally involves pulling foods apart so that a young person can feel what the food is like inside. As they are doing this, you can ask questions such as:

- What does it feel like in your hand?

- Does it feel as you imagined it would? Better, worse?

- Can you imagine putting this in your mouth? (Tip: If the answer to this is 'no', it might be time to start over with a new food.)

- What do you think it will feel like in your mouth?

As the young person touches the food, this naturally exposes them to the smell of the food, and you can ask similar questions to those above about smell. Smell gives ideas about taste, and you can question them about that in the same way.

Cooking and handling the food, or being around other people eating it, also provides a staged process of desensitisation prior to actually trying the food.

Staged desensitisation

1. Choose the food using visual examples from the internet or magazines.
2. Look at the food in a real-world situation – for example, a café or supermarket.
3. Buy the food.
4. Prepare and cook the food (if necessary).
5. Sit next to someone eating the food.
6. Touch and handle the food.
7. Smell the food.

Once a young person has desensitised to a new food, they are ready to work on the anxiety associated with trying it.

Managing anxiety

Anxiety is a major part of ARFID, and it can be very evident in the older age group. Older children and teenagers experience not only anxieties and fears about foods but also frequently an awareness of being 'different' and embarrassment about eating. The good news is that young people of this age group can develop the skills necessary to manage anxiety and cope with stressful eating situations.

We saw in Chapter 2 that when we are anxious or fearful, our brain triggers the 'fight or flight' response which gets the body ready for action. This leads to a number of physical changes in the body, such as increased heart rate, faster breathing, tense muscles, slowing of digestion and heightened senses. These reactions are all very useful if we actually have to fight something or run away, but not if the threat is perceived or imaginary. Anxiety contains four connected elements – thoughts, body changes, behaviours and feelings – all of which play a part.

Elements of anxiety

Imagine you have been invited to a party but find social occasions very difficult. Before the party you start to think (thought) that you will make a fool of yourself. Your heart races and you feel sick (body changes), so you text the host and tell them you can't go (behaviour), but then worry (feeling) that you will have upset them.

Now, imagine you have made it to the party. The host approaches you with a plate of food and you start to panic (feeling), in case they offer you food you can't eat (thought). Your mouth goes dry and you need to go to the toilet (body changes). As a result, you make your excuses and leave (behaviour).

These responses are the modern-day equivalent of 'fight or flight', but unfortunately they make handling the anxious situation harder, particularly when it comes to eating. Teaching young people to tackle the elements of anxiety – in particular, thoughts, body changes and behaviour – can lead to a reduction in the feelings of worry, stress and panic. This helps them try new foods and manage social eating situations, both of which increase their independence around foods and mealtimes.

Tackling anxious thoughts

A commonly used approach for anxious thoughts is cognitive behavioural therapy (CBT). This is usually provided by a clinical psychologist or other suitably trained mental health professional. CBT is a 'talking therapy' based on the idea that when we are anxious our thoughts become distorted, negative and out of control. By challenging these distorted and negative thoughts, we can prevent feelings of anxiety or panic taking hold. This can be done by looking at the evidence for the thought, challenging the thought and replacing it with a more positive one.

Challenging anxious thinking
The following stepped approach can help a young person with ARFID challenge anxious thoughts about eating. For example:

Thought: That food will make me sick.

Evidence: Other people are eating it, and they are not being sick.

Challenge: It's unlikely I'll be sick.

Positive: I can spit it out if I want, and I might even like it!

Challenging anxious thinking can be difficult with autistic children and teenagers. This is because they generally find it very difficult to imagine alternative ways of looking at a problem due to their difficulties with social imagination. When a young person is faced with a new food that they want to try, but are very nervous about, a really useful question to ask is 'What is the worst that can happen?' You are likely to get answers such as, 'It will make me sick' or 'It might poison me' or 'I might die.' They might even say, 'I don't know.' This is because we are not always consciously aware of our disgust responses. Helping the young person to work out alternative outcomes or solutions – for example, 'I can spit it out if I don't like it' – can help.

Tackling body changes

Some young people with ARFID, even very able ones, can find these thought challenges very hard indeed. This is because the fear associated with foods is very strong. For them, tackling the body changes that occur during anxiety using relaxation techniques is more effective.

Relaxation techniques are simple and can be used anywhere. Regular practice lowers overall anxiety and helps young people generally cope better. Some techniques, such as deep breathing and muscle relaxation, are easily done at home and there are many readily available resources for young people such as CDs or mobile phone apps to help them. Some techniques usually require additional professional help, so if you are a parent, approach your GP for a referral. A clinical psychologist or other mental health professional can teach visualisation techniques, and a qualified and registered hypnotherapist can provide hypnotherapy. We have found that many parents also benefit themselves from practising relaxation with their child or teenager as it is a great all-round stress buster! Relaxation used immediately before trying a new food helps lower the anxiety associated with eating something different and can allow the young person to successfully have their first taste.

Which technique?
There are three main forms of relaxation:

1. diaphragmatic breathing
2. progressive muscle relaxation
3. visualisation.

Individuals respond differently to each technique, so it is best to try all three and see which is best. To work this out, record anxiety levels before and after practising each relaxation technique using a numbered scale – for example, 0–10, where 0 is minimum anxiety and 10 is maximum anxiety. This also keeps a record of progress. Using visual scales is a good idea for autistic young people.

When we are anxious or stressed, our breathing is shallow and faster. Breathing deeply and slowly using the diaphragm (the part of the body which separates the chest and the abdomen) slows the heart rate and calms other body changes that occur when we are anxious. For young people, it is a great emergency 'calm down' technique that can be used by them anywhere.

Deep breathing exercise

1. Place one hand on your chest and the other on your stomach.
2. Breathe in through your nose counting to three. If you are breathing deeply, the hand that is on your stomach should rise up. This is because the diaphragm is contracting and moving to allow more air into the lungs.
3. Breathe out through your nose or mouth counting to three. The hand on your stomach should go down. This is because the diaphragm is relaxing and pushing the air out of the lungs.
4. Repeat this ten times.

When we are anxious, our muscles become tense and relaxing muscles helps the whole body feel calmer. To learn the difference between 'tense' and 'relaxed', hold a stress ball (available in many toy and budget shops) in the hand and squeeze tightly (but not so tightly it hurts) for five seconds and then release. This can also be a quick and discreet relaxation technique for young people to do themselves.

Progressive muscle relaxation exercises work by tensing and relaxing different muscle groups around the body in turn. It is a good technique for young people who find imagination exercises difficult. When doing a muscle relaxation exercise, it is important for the individual to go at their own pace and only tense the muscles gently and not so hard that they hurt.

Progressive muscle relaxation exercise

1. Find a quiet place sitting comfortably or lying down.
2. Take ten deep breaths (see 'Deep breathing exercise' above).
3. Squeeze your hands into fists and tense for three seconds, then release.
4. Bend your arms and touch your shoulders and tense for three seconds, then release.
5. Hunch your shoulders up to your ears and tense for three seconds, then release.
6. Shut your eyes tightly and tense for three seconds, then release.
7. Tense the muscles in your stomach for three seconds, then release.
8. Point your toes downward and tense for three seconds, then release.
9. Point your toes upward and tense for three seconds, then release.
10. When you are ready, get up slowly. Never jump up quickly after a relaxation exercise.

Visualisation, or imagining being in a calm and relaxing place, is a really good technique for young people who find it difficult to 'switch off' their anxious mind. We have also found it to be the most effective relaxation technique to help with eating, particularly when the visualisation script includes imagining eating a new food. The rationale is that if a young person can imagine trying or eating a new food while relaxed, it will be easier for them to do so in the 'real' world. For the most able young people, we use 'hypnotherapy' techniques. These include positive suggestions for new behaviour, such as being able to eat a new food.

Calm and relaxing scripts

Young people must always be in control of what goes into their visualisation scripts. I once wrote a script about walking barefoot on a beach which made the young person even more anxious as they hated the feel of sand! For autistic young people who find tasks involving imagination difficult, suggestions and visual aids can get them started:

- Use a real place – for example, a holiday.
- Use visual aids such as photographs or drawings.
- Give suggestions – for example, beach, forest, lake.
- Avoid scenarios in video games– these are generally not relaxing!

Tackling behaviour

When a young person with ARFID is in 'fight or flight' mode about eating, they might avoid a mealtime altogether. Avoiding an anxiety-provoking situation, such as trying a new food or going to a party where they might be offered food, is a very common behaviour in young people with ARFID. We tackle this by helping them learn and practise new behaviours around food – first in a structured way, away from mealtimes, and then transferring these skills into mealtimes at home and into other social eating situations.

Taste trials

A taste trial is a structured and step-by-step process to trying a new food. It teaches a new behaviour and gives the young person more independence over their eating. In particular, it lets them – perhaps for the first time – choose what to try, when to do it and whether to do it again. Before beginning a taste trial, it is important that the young person is ready. This includes being motivated, which increases with age. Even autistic young people who struggle with social skills can be influenced by their peers as they get older. Motivation also helps in choosing which foods to try. A highly motivating food is often one that friends eat, or one that can be eaten on a school trip or family holiday. However, it must be the young person's choice and not the adult's.

Taste trials

Charlie has ARFID and autism. When he was 16, I taught him some relaxation techniques and went on to several taste trials, not all of which were successful (the disastrous rice pudding trial sticks in my mind!). However, Charlie didn't give up – in fact, as he got older, he took the techniques and used them when he was ready. Recently, Charlie turned 18 and celebrated by going to a pizza restaurant, which was the first time his family had been able to eat out together and was a momentous occasion! Charlie also told me that he was 'sure' he could eat pizza on his 18th birthday outing because there was a girl coming who 'might become his girlfriend'. This only increased Charlie's determination to eat pizza!

Another way of choosing a new food is to pick one that is very similar to one already eaten (see 'Spreading the sets' in Chapter 10). This is particularly good for young people who are lacking in confidence about their ability to try something new as it gives them the best chance of success. I have found that choosing one or two new foods at a time is enough; more than this and it becomes difficult to desensitise and slowly learn to like the new foods.

Having a reward immediately after trying the food can also help; this acts as an additional motivator. The reward should be tangible and meaningful to the young person, such as extra computer time. Stickers and reward charts are generally ineffective, as these are not enough to overcome the disgust and anxiety responses and are generally too abstract and not age-appropriate for ARFID teenagers. In addition, food rewards should not be used.

> **Why not reward with foods?**
> A reward should not be another food. Consider the message we are giving when we reward a child for eating one food with another. The classic example is 'Eat up your greens, and then you can have your pudding.' By saying this, what we are actually doing is decreasing the value of the food to be eaten up (the greens) and increasing the value of the food to be had next (the pudding). What we should really be saying if we want children to eat more greens is 'Eat up your pudding and then you can have your greens'!

A taste trial can be done at home with a parent or other adult (preferably one who is not so stressed about eating) or with a professional, particularly if they have been involved in teaching CBT or relaxation. A trial should always be done away from the pressures of mealtimes. Rating the food is important, as it will help the young person decide (and remember) what they thought about the food. It takes around ten tastes before we learn to like a new food and include it in our diets, so regular trials, such as every day or several times a week, give the best chance of success. The following are some general principles of a taste trial:

- Choose a food for the trial that the young person has agreed to try.
- Schedule the trial for the least stressful time of the day or week.
- Provide a bin for spitting out the food if necessary.

- Practise a preferred relaxation technique immediately before the trial.

- Taste a small amount – a 1cm cube is enough.

- Reward immediately after trying the food.

- Provide a favourite drink after the trial.

- Rate the food – for example, on a scale of 0–10.

- Repeat the trial with the same food regularly.

Recording what a young person thinks of a new food is very important. It helps them decide (and remember) whether they like it and monitors progress from trial to trial, including whether the food is increasing in value. Regular practice is also important as it is not the first taste that is the hardest but the second! This is because the young person has to slowly learn to like the new food, and by the second taste they have a more realistic sense of what the food is actually like. It is therefore important to maintain momentum and motivation by scheduling trials and rewards. In order to increase motivation for the second taste, it may be necessary to save a slightly bigger reward for this one and not the first. If the first, second and third tastes are getting low ratings (of 3 or less), it may be better to start the process again with a different food.

Becoming independent

Once a young person has tried, and begun to like a new food, they can begin to include the food in their diet at mealtimes at home and in other 'real-world' eating situations such as school or college. In addition, all of the techniques discussed in this chapter can be used to help an older child or teenager with ARFID manage social eating situations. For example, visiting a café is a great natural desensitisation technique, even if nothing is eaten, and deep breathing can be practised discreetly before sitting with friends to eat.

All of these strategies rely on the young person having some motivation to move on. However, we have yet to meet a young person in this more able group where this hasn't happened.

It is simply a matter of time and waiting until they are ready. Once they are ready, these strategies can increase independence and autonomy around eating. This is a theme we will return to in our final chapter.

> As Rebecca got older, she learnt how to add foods into her diet one at a time. One of these foods was a particular flavour and brand of Cornish pasty. When she chose a university, Rebecca picked one that had an onsite branch of the outlet that sold her favourite pasty. That way she could always access her favourite foods without having to draw unnecessary attention to her eating difficulties.

Summary

- Motivation is the key to helping older children and teenagers move on.

- Desensitisation and managing sensory overload helps older children and teenagers manage their own sensory issues around foods.

- Older children and teenagers can learn skills for managing anxiety around foods, and can help them try a new food or manage social eating situations.

- Anxiety can be managed by tackling anxious thoughts and body changes using visualisation and practising new behaviours around foods.

- Taste trials are a structured way for young people to learn how to try new foods.

- It can take up to ten tastes for a new food to be liked, so it is important to schedule regular trials.

- Once a young person has learnt to like a new food in a taste trial, they can then include it in their diet at home and in social eating situations in the real world.

- Learning to manage eating in real-world settings increases independence and autonomy around foods.

. . .

Tips for parents and carers

- Always allow your child their preferred foods, particularly during stressful and anxious times.
- Encourage your child to use desensitisation and strategies for managing sensory overload themselves.
- Help your child in learning to manage their anxiety; this might include seeking professional help.
- Experiment with different relaxation techniques and find the one that works for your child.
- Schedule regular and achievable times for taste trials.
- When trying new foods, only work on one or two foods at a time.
- Keep a record of progress, including what new foods have been tried and/or added to the diet.
- Provide the young person with opportunities to transfer their new skills to real-world eating situations – for example, going out with friends to a café or restaurant.

. . .

Chapter 12

What Else Might Be Going Wrong?

Where have we got to?

So far, we have concentrated on those children and young people who present with a particular eating difficulty, namely a restricted diet and a fearful response to new foods. This pattern of eating is now described using the diagnostic label 'Avoidant and Restrictive Food Intake Disorder' or 'ARFID'. We have seen how this develops through a combination of linked factors in development which include sensory hypersensitivity, neophobia, disgust and anxiety and which leads to a learned safety in the choice of foods. We have also seen how ARFID can occur in children with or without autism. Part 2 of this book has described evidence- and practice-based interventions suitable across the spectrum of ARFID eating behaviours.

However, for some children and young people, ARFID may not be the whole story. This is particularly true for those on the autism spectrum. This last chapter will look at other eating difficulties that can present alongside ARFID and/or autism. It will cover the role of other eating disorders, the impact of pathological demand avoidance (PDA), the role of mental health issues such as obsessive-compulsive disorder and depression, and the eating of non-foods, or pica. It will end with a section on managing ARFID in the transition to adulthood.

Eating disorders

> When Rosie was 14, she began to restrict her eating. To begin with, nobody noticed as Rosie preferred wearing baggy and loose clothes anyway, but after six months it was more obvious that she was losing weight. By the time she was 15, Rosie was very underweight and was admitted to an eating disorder unit for adolescents, where she was given a diagnosis of anorexia nervosa.

The eating disorder anorexia nervosa is characterised by a restriction in calorie intake due to a desire to control weight and an intense fear of becoming fat. This is usually combined with a disturbance in the way in which body weight or shape is experienced. Typically, individuals with anorexia think they are bigger and heavier than they actually are. It can be a very dangerous condition and is generally associated with other mental health issues. It occurs more frequently in females and often begins in the teenage years.

Since the introduction of the ARFID label, researchers have become interested in comparing ARFID with anorexia. In both eating patterns there are similarities, which include the risk of being underweight and high levels of anxiety, but also differences, such as ARFID being more common in males and being more likely to coexist with developmental disorders such as autism. Some of these similarities and differences are detailed in Table 12.1.

Table 12.1 Similarities and differences between
ARFID and anorexia nervosa

ARFID	Anorexia nervosa
Fear of the different/ neophobic response	Fear of fatness
Sensory hypersensitivity	The need to control weight
Visual sensitivity	The need to control diet to 'healthy' norms
Unlikely vegetables/likely beige carbohydrates	Restriction to healthy and low-calorie foods
Risk of being underweight	Extreme underweight
Seen more in males	Seen more in females
Occurs frequently in autism	Occurs more frequently in autism

In addition, research has also found some possible links between anorexia and autism. For example, in both conditions, rigid and inflexible thinking appears to play a part and, in particular, teenage girls with anorexia have been found to have higher than expected levels of traits associated with autism (Baron-Cohen *et al.* 2013).

This appeared to be the case for Rosie. After she had been in the eating disorder unit for a couple of weeks, staff noticed some differences between her and the other residents. These included that she didn't seem to want to lose weight, had sensory issues and was more rigid and fixed on routines. Rosie was assessed by a psychologist and was given a diagnosis of Asperger's syndrome and also of ARFID.

There is some research evidence that autistic females are more at risk of developing serious problems with eating than their non-autistic peers (Huke *et al.* 2013). It is also the case that autistic females can have elements of more than one type of eating difficulty. This does not mean that every girl or woman on the spectrum will develop an eating problem, but managing the risks is very important. This includes understanding why these eating problems develop – for example, the restriction to certain foods in ARFID because of sensory sensitivity and learned safety as opposed to the restriction of calories to control weight in anorexia.

Rosie's eating issues began in her teenage years which she found very stressful, particularly when managing friendships. For her, restricting her eating was not about losing weight but was a way of coping with this anxiety. Rosie herself gave me one of the best descriptions of the differences between ARFID and anorexia I have ever heard:

> Every morning in the unit we would have toast and jam for breakfast. Afterwards I had to wash my hands; I couldn't stand them being sticky with jam. I soon noticed that other residents in the unit were doing the same, but this was because they were worried they would lick the jam from their fingers and get fat. (Rosie, aged 16)

It is important to recognise that many young people with autism and ARFID will restrict their intake during periods of stress and anxiety, but that this does not necessarily represent a desire to be thinner or reflect a distortion about the way they look. However, we must not overlook the risks of anorexia or other eating disorders either, particularly where the young person's social-communication differences may make it difficult for them to verbalise any body shape or weight concerns.

I have since met other autistic women with eating issues who have reported many different reasons for restricting foods and/or losing weight. These include fitting in with peers, developing a special interest in dieting and an intense identification and empathy with animals leading to vegetarianism or veganism. For many of these women, the control of eating became a way of controlling the anxiety associated with being 'different'.

If you are a concerned parent, seek specialist assessment and advice, preferably from a service that understands eating disorders in adolescence, including ARFID and the impact of autism. Managing anxiety is also crucial to prevent any eating issue getting worse. Again, seek support, for example from Child and Adolescent Mental Health Services (CAMHS).

Vegetarian and vegan diets

Restricting foods or whole food groups can take many forms, not all of which are 'disordered'. My husband is vegan. For him, this is an ethical choice, but he also reports that as a child he found the smell, taste and texture of meat disgusting. He still notices smells, noises and small details that others do not!

However, for those with anorexia, becoming vegetarian or vegan can be an effective method of reducing intake and calorie load, and this should be monitored closely. For young people with ARFID, the decision to drop whole food groups, such as meat or dairy, is usually more related to sensory sensitivities and disgust. For autistic young people, who experience additional difficulties with social skills, becoming vegetarian or vegan can also be due to a heightened emotional sensitivity to, or empathy with, animals.

Pathological demand avoidance

> Susie was 15 when she received her diagnosis of Asperger's syndrome. Susie had become more and more anxious in school and had eventually stopped attending. Her anxieties then transferred to home with Susie being unable to cope with even the smallest everyday demand or task and to engage in any activities outside of home.

The term 'pathological demand avoidance' (PDA) describes a group of behaviours seen in some young people with traits of, or a diagnosis of, autism. As such, it is now considered to be part of the autistic spectrum. These young people react to everyday demands and expectations with extreme avoidance behaviours, ranging from verbal refusal to escape and complete withdrawal. The demand-avoidant behaviour is rooted in an anxiety-based need to be in control. It is often extreme and can be very difficult to manage.

For some young people with PDA, eating becomes a 'demand' and can lead to highly controlled and specific rituals about how foods are chosen, prepared and eaten or the complete avoidance of mealtimes altogether. In Susie's case, she could not cope with the demand of choosing foods to eat herself and would only eat if her mum chose the foods for her. At times her PDA was so bad that her mum had to spoon-feed her.

We know that high levels of sensory hypersensitivity are often reported in young people with PDA, and this may play a similar role in PDA to the role it plays in ARFID. However, not all young people with demand-avoidant behaviour around food display all the classic characteristics of ARFID, such as brand loyalty or neophobia. However, it is likely that sensory sensitivities, extreme anxiety and a decrease in appetite are all playing a part. For these young people, PDA-friendly strategies and sensory and anxiety-based interventions around foods (see Chapters 10 and 11) are likely to be helpful.

PDA-friendly strategies

- Be flexible and balance tolerance and demands. On some days the child will be able to cope with more, on others less.

- Choose your battles. Is it worth a meltdown? Or is this a non-negotiable?

- Manage sensory overload (see Chapters 10 and 11).

- Manage anxiety and uncertainty using planners, schedules and visual aids.

- Use natural consequences – for example, 'When you've got your shoes on, we can go to the park' – rather than rewards or punishments.

PDA can be difficult to deal with, because although it is connected to the autism spectrum, it does not always respond to autism-friendly strategies. If you are a concerned parent, seek professional support from your GP or appropriate mental health services. When it comes to food, giving the young person back some control at their pace can be effective. For example, Susie's mother introduced a schedule for eating which gave Susie a daily menu with two options at each meal and snack time that she could choose from. This lowered the demand for Susie and meant she could cope a bit more.

Mental health

As we have seen throughout this book, anxiety plays a major role in the development and maintenance of ARFID. Are there other mental health issues that might coexist or be connected with an ARFID pattern of eating?

Obsessive-compulsive disorder

Obsessive-compulsive disorder (OCD) is a significant mental health problem, where the individual experiences frequent intrusive and unwelcome obsessional thoughts, often followed by compulsions, impulses or urges. These can result in repetitive behaviours designed to relieve the anxiety associated with the obsessional thoughts; however, this relief is usually short-lived. For example, Rosie reported that although her rituals around food shopping, preparation and eating helped her feel calm when she was actually doing them, the fact that she could not stop them made her more anxious.

There is some research evidence of an overlap between eating disorders such as anorexia or binge eating disorder and OCD, with the thoughts and behaviours around foods in these eating disorders having an obsessive and compulsive element to them. This research into adult 'picky eaters' has also reported higher OCD symptoms compared with 'non-picky' eaters. We do not know how OCD and eating disorders overlap; however, the research reports that adults with OCD and/or anorexia have a higher sensitivity to disgust, for example (Kauer *et al.* 2015).

There are also thought to be different types of OCD. One of these is persistent thoughts and fears about contamination. As we have seen, contamination responses and fears around foods are also common in young people with ARFID and are related to sensory sensitivities and disgust (see Chapter 4).

Alex, aged 17, has ARFID and some autistic traits. He worries that many foods are 'poisonous' and has contamination fears about utensils and is only able to use one plate and one cup that he has decided are safe. If these touch other utensils, or are washed up in the same water, Alex cannot touch or use them. Alex also has to wash his plate and cup ten times each time he uses them. These worries and behaviours developed when he started sixth form.

Obsessive behaviours are also commonly reported in autism, although may differ from OCD in their origin, perhaps being more related to the cognitive rigidity and the 'desire for sameness' seen in the condition. Distinguishing between the obsessive behaviours seen in autism and the mental health problem of OCD can be difficult, particularly where the young person is non-verbal. Again, if you are a concerned parent, seek professional help, particularly if the obsessive behaviours are having a negative impact on the young person and family life.

Depression

Many younger children I speak to in clinic are happy with their eating pattern, are unaware of their differences and have no desire to change. However, when I speak to teenagers or young adults with ARFID, many of them report the negative impact their eating pattern has on them – they show real problems with psycho-social functioning.

This impact can occur in a number of ways. Research with adult picky eaters shows that they score more highly than non-picky eaters on measures of depression, and quality-of-life impairment such as greater social anxiety related to eating (Kauer *et al.* 2015). This is certainly the case for many young people with ARFID, where their food anxiety generalises and leads to a social anxiety about eating away from home. Unfortunately, withdrawing from social occasions which might involve eating has an additional and negative impact, as it stops the young person from experiencing environmental rewards, such as enjoyment from being out with friends. This only serves to make the anxiety and mood issues worse. In addition, persistent and chronic anxiety can also lead to depression.

Mental health in autism

Mental health problems are unfortunately very common in autistic young people. This is thought to be due to a combination of factors which lead to a vulnerability to stress. These include thinking and sensory differences, social difficulties and isolation, problems of self-esteem and confidence, and difficulties thinking flexibly and problem solving. In addition, autistic young people may not be able to adequately recognise, communicate and cope with their feelings, particularly if they are not verbal.

Able autistic young people may also hide or 'mask' their difficulties, so it may not always be obvious that they are depressed or anxious. The analogy of the swan is useful here. The swan appears to glide effortlessly and serenely across the water; however, what we can't see underneath the water is the fast and furious paddling of its feet! It is the same for some autistic young people – just because they seem okay on the outside does not mean that they are not coping on the inside.

Mental health issues can show themselves first in changes in behaviour and then in changes of mood. For example, the young person may have sleeping problems, further restrict their foods or withdraw from usual activities. It is important therefore that mental health issues in young people are identified as early as possible and treated. If you are a concerned parent, seek professional help from your GP or specialist Child and Adolescent Mental Health Services (CAMHS).

Pica

Billy has autism and a learning disability. He regularly eats the paint off the walls at school, plastic toys and bark chippings in the playground. School staff distract him and try to replace the items he eats with safe alternatives such as a 'chew-buddy' and chopped raw vegetables that he can munch on instead.

Pica (which is the Latin name for 'magpie') is the persistent eating of non-nutritive or non-food items. Common items eaten include soil, paper, cloth, plants, plastic, chalk, paint, hair and wood. We do not know why individuals display pica; however, it is reported across the world and throughout history. It does appear to be more common in people with a learning or intellectual disability and in autism. We also don't know why pica happens; however, one theory is that pica is connected to sensory issues and that non-food items are eaten because of the rewarding sensory consequences of consuming the pica item itself. In addition, pica is often reported to increase during times of stress, so anxiety or arousal levels may also play a part. Interestingly, pica is also seen in young people with ARFID, not all of whom have autism. Some researchers have noted this overlap and speculated that both conditions involve an intense focus (or 'obsession') on a few foods (in ARFID) or on non-food items (in pica).

Pica carries significant health risks; which include poisoning, oral and dental health problems, infections, intestinal obstruction and gut or bowel perforation. In addition, pica can be very serious with one pica incident, such as eating something poisonous, being enough to cause significant harm or even death. Risk management, including careful consideration of the items eaten and what harm these could cause, is therefore very important. If you are a parent of a child or young person with pica, it is very important that you seek professional support, particularly in monitoring their health.

Managing pica

The number-one priority in pica is to keep the young person safe. This includes monitoring for dangerous pica items which can cause an immediate risk of harm or death such as choking, poisoning or gut perforation. However, other materials may cause more long-term and chronic problems such as infections, blockages in the stomach and bowel (known as 'bezoars') or general ill-health.

It is important that a young person with pica has regular health checks which might include blood tests, scans and physical examinations. It is also important to remember that autistic, non-verbal young people may not display signs of ill-health, such as pain or discomfort, in the same way as other young people. Providing a 'pica-box' of safe alternatives to mouth or eat and distracting young people with favourite activities are good strategies to reduce pica. An occupational therapy assessment can help with understanding the young person's sensory issues.

Transition to adulthood

We do not know how many adults have ARFID. Research studies on adults with picky eating (which may be similar to ARFID) have identified some similarities between this eating pattern in childhood and in adulthood which include rejecting particular tastes or textures, disliking mixed foods or food touching and concerns about the availability of foods at social occasions (Ellis *et al.* 2017). Given that the factors involved in ARFID, such as sensory hypersensitivity, neophobia and disgust, are mostly 'inborn' traits, it seems likely that ARFID will also persist, at least to some degree, into adulthood. Certainly, for those young people on the autism spectrum, whose differences are most likely to be life-long, eating problems frequently continue into adulthood.

> Louisa is now 18 and transitioning to adult autism and learning disability services. She continues to have ARFID. She has become anxious about the

transition and has begun to lose weight again. Adult services want her to adopt a 'healthy eating' plan and to reduce her intake of crisps and chocolate. Louisa's mother, Anne, is educating the professionals involved about ARFID, particularly the need to allow her preferred foods as she goes through the stressful transitional period.

A change to eating patterns doesn't just happen when the young person turns 18! This is particularly true for those on the autism spectrum, who have social and emotional skills that are usually several years behind their non-autistic peers. However, even for these young people, the motivation to change and the skills necessary to do so can still develop, albeit slowly. Managing eating and becoming gradually independent can therefore be a slow process and involves continuing to apply appropriate strategies and getting support from services that understand the eating pattern.

As the diagnosis of ARFID has become more widely known, we have received more calls and emails from adults who now recognise that this label applies to them. Many of these adults report wanting to change their eating pattern because of the negative impact it is having on their life. For example, Will, who has just become a father, is now highly motivated for the first time to change his eating because he doesn't want his son growing up with a dad who is a 'fussy eater'. Will recently got a job as a chef in a restaurant, which has had a very positive (and, for him, unexpected) impact on his ARFID.

> I didn't tell anyone at work about my ARFID when I landed the job, I just had to get on with it. This meant I had to touch and prepare foods I hadn't even seen before and deal with all the smells in the kitchen. I thought I'd find it really hard, but it was okay and now new foods don't bother me so much anymore. I can even eat some of the dishes on the menu! I've even been able to eat there with my family which was brilliant. (Will, age 22)

This just goes to prove the impact on ARFID of desensitisation! For Will, however, it really helped that he was motivated to make a success of his new job. As we have seen, motivation increases with age and leads to a greater chance of being able to make some changes, particularly when it comes to eating new foods. Another important step is the young person taking more responsibility and becoming more independent in the choice, preparation and cooking of their preferred foods. For Dan, a bit like Will, this came along naturally with a change in his circumstances.

> Mum has always cooked my foods, I'm just used to her doing that, but it all changed when I got my evening job, as she's still at work when I have to eat my tea and then get to work. I'm learning to cook chicken nuggets myself now. I use the timer on my mobile so I know exactly how long they need to be in the oven to be the right shade of brown. (Dan, age 21)

Managing the social consequences of having ARFID is also another great leap into independence. For many young people and adults with ARFID, social mealtimes have been avoided for years and have had an impact on their ability to make and maintain friendships. For some of these young people, particularly those on the autism spectrum, the 'rules' about social eating situations may need to be learnt, perhaps for the first time.

> **Learning the 'rules' of social eating**
> If you are an adult with problems eating, the following can help when eating away from home:
> - Explain to those you are eating with that you have difficulties with foods.
> - Ask what might be on the menu in advance if you are eating at a friend's house or whether you can bring some of your own foods with you.
> - Sit on the end of a table if you have strong disgust responses to other people's foods or watching them eating.
> - Plan your visit if going to a restaurant or café. You may be able to look at the menu on the internet, for example, or go and visit the restaurant first so you can decide what you might order and where you might sit.
> - Minimise sensory overload by going at a quiet time or using earplugs or headphones, or take a distraction, such as book, phone or tablet.

For adults with ARFID, the individual motivators for change are many and varied. However, almost always it is about being less anxious about foods, being able eat a bit more variety, being less embarrassed about eating and being able to do typical things, such as manage Christmas or eat out with family and friends. As Rebecca puts it, 'There were so many things I felt like my diet stopped me from doing, I just wanted to do them!'

Summary

- Some young people with ARFID have additional eating difficulties. This can be particularly true for those on the autism spectrum.

- Eating disorders such as anorexia can be more common in autism. They appear to be different from ARFID but some young people, particularly females, can show traits of both.

- PDA can cause a young person to become extremely anxious and controlling around foods or to avoid eating almost completely.

- Mental health issues such as OCD and depression appear to be more common in people with restricted diets. They are also more common in autism. Sensory sensitivities, disgust, rigidity and anxiety may all play a part.

- Pica can have serious life-threatening consequences, and the priority should always be to keep the young person safe and healthy.

- ARFID can persist into adulthood, particularly in those on the autism spectrum.

- Learning to become more independent around eating and social eating situations can have a very positive impact on the young person's life, particularly in the transition to adulthood.

. . .

Tips for parents and carers

- Seek professional help if you are concerned about an eating disorder, particularly if there has been unexplained weight loss.

- Use PDA-friendly strategies with young people to reduce demands and continue to use strategies for managing sensory sensitivities and anxiety to help with eating.

- Seek professional help if you are concerned about any mental health issue such as OCD or depression.

- Manage the health risks in pica, particularly if the pica items are potentially dangerous. Seek support from your GP or other health professional and provide safe alternatives to mouth or eat.

- Encourage independence in young people with ARFID by getting them involved in cooking and food preparation skills.
- Encourage and support opportunities for the young person with ARFID to participate in social eating situations.

. . .

Final Words

We have written this book in the hope that it helps parents, and those working with parents, who are struggling to understand why it is that their child just doesn't seem to want to eat.

All through our clinical practice it has been the parents who are most worried about food refusal, very rarely the child. The fear of food only becomes a problem for the child as they grow older; these issues can be seen in adults as well as children. Only then does it make life difficult. How can I eat out? How can I travel? How can I stay with friends? The strategies we have suggested throughout this book can therefore be used by adults as well as with children.

This area of research and intervention is still in its infancy but it is our hope that the field will continue to produce new and innovative ideas and strategies for helping those with a fear of food. We also hope that as ARFID becomes more widely understood, those coping with the condition will receive appropriate support and understanding to enable them to feel less isolated.

Bibliography

Chapter 1

Carruth, B.R. and Skinner J.D. (2002) 'Feeding behaviors and other motor development in healthy children (2–24 months).' *Journal of the American College of Nutrition 21*, 2, 88–96.

Coulthard, H., Harris, G., Emmet, P. and the ALSPAC team. (2010) 'Long term consequences of early fruit and vegetable feeding practices.' *Public Health and Nutrition 13*, 12, 2044–2051.

Fildes, A., van Jaarsveld, C., Cooke, L., Wardle, J. and Llewellyn, C. (2014) 'Common genetic architecture underlying young children's food fussiness and liking for vegetables and fruit.' *American Journal of Clinical Nutrition 99*, 4, 911–917.

Gisel, E.G. (1991) 'Effect of food texture on the development of chewing of children between six months and two years of age.' *Developmental Medicine and Child Neurology 33*, 1, 69–79.

Harris, G. and Mason, S. (2017) 'Are there sensitive periods for food acceptance in infancy?' *Current Nutrition Reports 6*, 2, 190–196.

Northstone, K., Emmett, P. and Nethersole, F. (2001) 'The effect of age of introduction to lumpy solids on foods eaten and reported feeding difficulties at 6 and 15 months.' *Journal of Human Nutrition and Dietetics 14*, 1, 43–54.

Ventura, A.K. and Woroby, J. (2013) 'Early influences on the development of food preferences.' *Current Biology 23*, 9, R401–R408.

Wardle, J. and Cooke, L. (2008) 'Genetic and environmental determinants of children's food preferences.' *British Journal of Nutrition 99*, S15–S21.

Chapter 2

Brown, S. and Harris, G. (2012) 'Rejection of known and previously accepted foods during early childhood: An extension of the neophobic response?' *International Journal of Child Health and Nutrition 1*, 1, 72–81.

Blissett, J., Bennett, C., Fogel, A., Harris, G. and Higgs, S. (2016) 'Parental modelling and prompting effects on acceptance of a novel fruit in 2–4-year-old children are dependent on children's food responsiveness.' *British Journal of Nutrition 115*, 3, 554–564.

Cooke, L., Wardle, J. and Gibson, E. (2003) 'Relationship between parental report of food neophobia and everyday food consumption in 2–6-year-old children.' *Appetite 41*, 2, 205–206.

Cooke, L.J., Haworth, C.M.A. and Wardle, J. (2007) 'Genetic and environmental influences on children's food neophobia.' *American Journal of Clinical Nutrition 86*, 2, 428–433.

Coulthard, H. and Sealy, A. (2017) 'Play with your food! Sensory play is associated with tasting of fruits and vegetables in preschool children.' *Appetite 113*, 84–90.

Farrow, C.V. and Coulthard, H. (2012) 'Relationships between sensory sensitivity, anxiety and selective eating in children.' *Appetite 58*, 3, 842–846.

Hendy, H.M. (2002) 'Effectiveness of trained peer models to encourage food acceptance in preschool children.' *Appetite 39*, 3, 217–225.

Holley, C.E., Haycraft, E. and Farrow, C. (2015) '"Why don't you try it again?" A comparison of parent led, home based interventions aimed at increasing children's consumption of a disliked vegetable.' *Appetite 87*, 215–222.

Rioux, C., Lafraire, J. and Picard, D. (2018) 'Visual exposure and categorization performance positively influence 3- to 6-year-old children's willingness to taste unfamiliar vegetables.' *Appetite 120*, 32–42.

Chapter 3

Coulthard H. and Blissett, J. (2009) 'Fruit and vegetable consumption in children and their mothers: Moderating effects of child sensory sensitivity.' *Appetite 52*, 2, 410–415.

Coulthard, H., Harris, G. and Fogel, A. (2016) 'Association between tactile over-responsivity and vegetable consumption early in the introduction of solid foods and its variation with age.' *Maternal and Child Nutrition 12*, 4, 848–859.

Monnery-Patris, S., Wagner, S., Rigal, N., Schwart, C. *et al*. (2015) 'Smell differential reactivity, but not taste differential reactivity, is related to food neophobia in toddlers.' *Appetite 95*, 303–309.

Nederkoorn, C., Jansen, A. and Havermans, R.C. (2015) 'Feel your food. The influence of tactile sensitivity on picky eating in children.' *Appetite 84*, 7–10.

Werthmann, J., Jansen, A., Havermans, R., Nederkoorn, C., Kremers, S. and Roefs, A. (2015) 'Bits and pieces. Food texture influences food acceptance in young children.' *Appetite 84*, 181–187.

Chapter 4

Batsell, R.W., Brown, A.S., Ansfield, M.E. and Paschall, G.Y. (2002) 'You will eat all of that! A retrospective analysis of forced consumption episodes.' *Appetite 38*, 3, 211–219.

Brown, S. and Harris, G. (2012) 'Disliked food acting as a contaminant during infancy. A disgust based motivation for rejection.' *Appetite 58*, 2, 535–558.

Kauer, J., Pelchat, M.L., Rozin, P. and Zickgraf, H.F. (2015) 'Adult picky eating. Phenomenology, taste sensitivity, and psychological correlates.' *Appetite 90*, 219–228.

Martin, Y. and Pliner, P. (2006) 'Ugh; that's disgusting. Identifying the characteristics of foods underlying rejections based on disgust.' *Appetite 46*, 1, 75–85.

Pliner, P., Eng, A. and Krishnan, K. (1995) 'The effects of fear and hunger on food neophobia in humans.' *Appetite 25*, 1, 77–87.

Chapter 5

Fisher, J.O. (2007) 'Effects of age on children's intake of large and self-selected food portions.' *Obesity 15*, 2, 403–412.

Fomon, S.J., Filer, L.J., Thomas, L., Anderson, T.A. and Nelson, S.E. (1975) 'Influence of formula concentration on caloric intake and growth of normal infants.' *Acta Paediatric Scandinavica 64*, 2, 172–181.

Lumeng, J.C. and Burke, L.M. (2006) 'Maternal prompts to eat, child compliance, and mother and child weight status.' *Journal of Pediatrics 149*, 3, 330–335.

McCrickerd, K., Leong, C. and Forde, C. (2017) 'Preschool children's sensitivity to teacher-served portion size is linked to age related differences in leftovers.' *Appetite 114*, 320–328.

Rolls, B.J., Engell, D. and Birch, L.L. (2000) 'Serving portion size influences 5-year-old but not 3-year-old children's food intakes.' *Journal of the American Dietetic Association 100*, 2, 232–234.

Widdowson, E.M. (1951) 'Mental contentment and physical growth.' *Lancet 1*, 6668, 1316–1318.

Chapter 6

American Psychiatric Association (2013*) Diagnostic and Statistical Manual of Mental Disorders* (5th edition). Arlington, VA: American Psychiatric Publishing.

Bryant-Waugh, R. (2013) 'Avoidant and restrictive food intake disorder: An illustrative case example.' *The International Journal of Eating Disorders 46*, 5, 420–423.

Coulthard, H. and Harris, G. (2003) 'Early food refusal: The role of maternal mood.' *Journal of Reproductive and Infant Psychology 21*, 335–345.

Maier, A., Chabanet, C., Schaal, B., Issanchou, S. and Leathwood, P. (2007) 'Effects of repeated exposure on acceptance of initially disliked vegetables in 7-month old infants.' *Food Quality and Preference 18*, 1023–1032.

Mason, S.J., Harris, G. and Blissett, J. (2005) 'Tube feeding in infancy: Implications for the development of normal eating and drinking skills.' *Dysphagia 20*, 46–61.

Smith, A.M., Roux, S., Naidoo, N.T. and Venter, D.J.L. (2005) 'Food choices of tactile defensive children.' *Nutrition 21*, 1, 14–19.

Chapter 7

Budd, K.S., McGraw, T.E., Farbisz, R., Murphy, T.B. *et al.* (1992) 'Psychosocial concomitants of children's feeding disorders.' *Journal of Paediatric Psychology 17*, 1, 81–94.

Craig, G.M., Scambler, G. and Spitz, L. (2003) 'Why parents of children with neurodevelopmental disabilities requiring gastrostomy feeding need more support.' *Developmental Medicine and Child Neurology 45*, 3, 183–188.

Crist, W., McDonnell, P. and Beck, M. (1994) 'Behaviour at mealtimes and the young child with cystic fibrosis.' *Journal of Developmental and Behavioural Pediatrics 15*, 157–161.

Greer, A.J., Gulotta, C.S., Masler, E.A. and Laud, R.B. (2008) 'Caregiver stress and outcomes of children with paediatric feeding disorders treated in an intensive interdisciplinary programme.' *Journal of Paediatric Psychology 33*, 6, 612–620.

HM Government (2016) *Childhood Obesity: A Plan for Action.* London: HM Government.

Postorino, V., Sanges, V., Giovagnoli, G., Fatta, L.M. *et al.* (2015) 'Clinical differences in children with autism spectrum disorder with and without food selectivity.' *Appetite 92*, 126–132.

Timini, S., Douglas, J. and Tsiftsopoulou, K. (1997) 'Selective eaters: A retrospective case note study.' *Child Care Health and Development 23*, 3, 265–278.

Chapter 8

Davis, A.M., Bruce, A.S., Khasawneh, R., Schulz, T., Fox, C. and Dunn, W. (2013) 'Sensory processing issues in young children presenting to an outpatient feeding clinic.' *Journal of Pediatric Gastroenterology and Nutrition 56*, 156–160.

Dunn, W. (1997) 'The impact of sensory processing abilities on the daily lives of young children and their families. A conceptual model.' *Infants and Young Children 9*, 23–35.

Klintwall, L., Fernell, E., Holm, A. and Gillberg, C. (2011) 'Sensory abnormalities in autism.' *Research in Developmental Disabilities 32*, 795–800.

Leekham, S.R., Nieto, C., Libby, S.J., Wing, L. and Gould, J. (2007) 'Describing the sensory abnormalities of children and adults with autism.' *Journal of Autism and Developmental Disorders 37*, 894–910.

Nadon, G., Feldman, D.E., Dunn, W. and Gisel, E. (2011) 'Association of sensory processing and eating problems in children with autism spectrum disorders.' *Autism Research and Treatment*, 2011, 1–8.

Chapter 9

Cooke, L.J., Chambers, L.C., Anez, E.V. and Wardle, J. (2011) 'Facilitating or undermining? The effect of reward on food acceptance. A narrative review.' *Appetite 57*, 493–497.

Frith, U. and Happé, F. (1994) 'Autism beyond "theory of mind".' *Cognition 50*, 115–132.

Galloway, A.T., Fiorito, L.M., Francis, L.A. and Birch, L.L. (2006) '"Finish your soup": Counterproductive effects of pressuring children to eat on intake and effect.' *Appetite 46*, 318–323.

Harris, G. and Booth, I.W. (1992) 'The Nature and Management of Eating Problems in Pre-school Children.' In P.J. Cooper and A. Stein (eds) *Feeding Problems and Eating Disorders in Children and Adolescents*. Monographs in Clinical Paediatrics. Chur: Harwood Academic.

Lopez, C., Tchanturia, K., Stahl, D. and Treasure, J. (2008) 'Central coherence in eating disorders: A systematic review.' *Psychological Medicine 38*, 10, 1393–1404.

Powell, F., Farrow, C. and Meyer, C. (2011) 'Food avoidance behaviours in children. The influence of maternal feeding practices and behaviours.' *Appetite 57*, 3, 683–692.

Chapter 10

Bogdashina, O. (2016) *Sensory Perceptual Issues in Autism and Asperger's Syndrome*. London: Jessica Kingsley Publishers.

Martins, Y., Young, R. and Robson, D. (2008) 'Feeding and eating behaviors in children with autism and typically developing children.' *Journal of Autism and Developmental Disorders 38*, 10, 1878–1887.

Nadon, G., Feldman, D.E., Dunn, W. and Gisel, E. (2011) 'Mealtime problems in children with autism spectrum disorder and their typically developing siblings: A comparison study.' *Autism 15*, 1, 98–113.

Nederkoorn, C., Theißen, J., Tummers, M. and Roefs, A. (2018) 'Taste the feeling or feel the tasting: Tactile exposure to food texture promotes food acceptance.' *Appetite 120*, 297–301.

Plaisted, K. (2001) 'Reduced Generalization in Autism: An Alternative to Weak Central Coherence.' In J.A. Burack, T. Charman, N. Yirmiya and P.R. Zelazo (eds) *The Development of Autism: Perspectives from Theory and Research*. Mahwah, NJ: Lawrence Erlbaum Associates.

Plaisted, K., Swettenham, J. and Rees, L. (1999) 'Children with autism show local precedence in a divided attention task and global precedence in a selective attention task.' *Journal of Child Psychology and Psychiatry 40*, 5, 733–742.

Remington, A.M., Añez, E., Cooke, L.J. and Wardle, J. (2011) 'Tiny tastes: A home based intervention promoting acceptance of disliked vegetables.' *Appetite 57*, 2, 564–564.

Schreck, K.A., Williams, K. and Smith, A.F. (2004) 'A comparison of eating behaviours between children with and without autism.' *Journal of Autism and Developmental Disorders 34*, 433–438.

Chapter 11

Allirot, X., Maiz, E. and Urdaneta, E. (2018) 'Shopping for food with children: A strategy for directing their choices toward novel foods containing vegetables.' *Appetite 120*, 287–296.

Attwood, T. (2007) *The Complete Guide to Asperger's Syndrome*. London: Jessica Kingsley Publishers.

Lakkaluka, A., Geaghan, J., Zanovec, M., Pierce, S. and Tuuri, G. (2010) 'Ten tastes does improve the liking of disliked vegetables in older children, but the effect is stronger with a sweet tasting vegetable.' *Appetite 55*, 2, 226–231.

Lohaus, A. and Klein-Hessling, J. (2003) 'Relaxation in children: Effects of extended and intensified training.' *Psychology and Health 18*, 2, 237–249.

Payne, R.A. (2000) *Relaxation Techniques: A Practical Handbook for the Healthcare Professional.* London: Harcourt Publishers.

Ollendick, T.H. and King, J.A. (1998) 'Empirically supported treatments for children with phobic and anxiety disorders: Current status.' *Journal of Clinical Child Psychology 27*, 2, 156–167.

Soronoff, K., Attwood, T. and Hinton, S. (2005) 'A randomised controlled trial of a CBT intervention for anxiety in children with Asperger's syndrome.' *Journal of Child Psychology and Psychiatry 46*, 11, 1152–1160.

Chapter 12

Baron-Cohen, S., Jaffa, T., Davies, S., Auyeung, B., Allison, C. and Wheelwright, S. (2013) 'Do girls with anorexia nervosa have elevated autistic traits?' *Molecular Autism 4*, 1, 24.

Ellis, J.M., Galloway, A.T., Webb, R.M. and Martz, D.M. (2017) 'Measuring adult picky eating: The development of a multidimensional self-report instrument.' *Psychological Assessment 29*, 8, 955–966.

Hagopian, L.P., Rooker, G.W. and Rolider, N.U. (2011) 'Identifying empirically supported treatments for pica in individuals with intellectual disabilities.' *Research in Developmental Disabilities 32*, 6, 2114–2120.

Hartman, A.S., Becker, A.E., Hampton, C. and Bryant-Waugh, R. (2012) 'Pica and rumination disorder in DSM-5.' *Psychiatric Annals 42*, 11, 426–430.

Huke, V., Turk, J., Saeidi, S., Kent, A. and Morgan, J.F. (2013) 'Autism spectrum disorders in eating disorder populations: A systematic review.' *European Eating Disorders Review 21*, 5, 345–351.

Kalyva, E. (2009) 'Comparison of eating attitudes between adolescent girls with and without AS: Daughters' and mothers' reports.' *Journal of Autism and Developmental Disorders 39*, 3, 480–486.

Kauer, J., Pelchat, M.L., Rozin, P. and Zickgraf, H.F. (2015) 'Adult picky eating. Phenomenology, taste sensitivity, and psychological correlates.' *Appetite 90*, 219–228.

Matson, J., Belva, B., Hattier, M.A. and Matson, M.L. (2011) 'Pica in persons with developmental disabilities: Characteristics, diagnosis and assessment.' *Research in Autism Spectrum Disorders 5*, 4, 1459–1464.

Matson, J., Hattier, M.A., Belva, B. and Matson, M.L. (2013) 'Pica in persons with developmental disabilities: Approaches to Treatment.' *Research in Developmental Disabilities 34*, 9, 2564–2571.

Newsom, E., Maréchal, K. and David, D. (2003) 'Pathological demand avoidance syndrome: A necessary distinction within the pervasive developmental disorders.' *Archives of Disease in Childhood 88*, 7, 595–600.

Nicely, T.A., Lane-Loney, S., Masciull, E., Hollenbeak, C.S. and Ornstein, R.M. (2014) 'Prevalence and characteristics of avoidant and restrictive food intake disorder in a cohort of young patients in day treatment for eating disorders.' *Journal of Eating Disorders 2*, 1, 21.

Norris, M.L., Robinson, A., Obeid, N., Harrison, M., Spettigue, W. and Henderson, K. (2013) 'Exploring avoidant/restrictive food intake disorder in eating disordered patients: A descriptive study.' *International Journal of Eating Disorders 47*, 5, 495–499.

Oldershaw, A., Treasure, J., Hambrook, D., Tchanturia, K. and Schmidt, U. (2011) 'Is anorexia nervosa a version of autism spectrum disorders?' *European Eating Disorders Review 19*, 6, 462–474.

Russell, A., Mataix Cols, D., Anson, M. and Murphy, D. (2005) 'Obsessions and compulsions in Asperger syndrome and high-functioning autism.' *British Journal of Psychiatry 186*, 525–528.

Stiegler, L.L. (2005) 'Understanding pica behaviour: A review for clinical and educational professionals.' *Focus on Autism and Developmental Disabilities 20*, 1, 27–38.

Sturmey, P. and Williams, D.E. (2016) *Pica in Individuals with Developmental Disabilities.* Switzerland: Springer International Publishing.

Resources

Beat – www.beateatingdisorders.org.uk

A UK based charity supporting anyone affected by eating disorders or any other difficulties with food, weight and shape.

Infant and Toddler Forum – www.infantandtoddlerforum.org

Provides evidence-based advice and simple, practical resources aimed at families and healthcare professionals in early years and child health.

The National Autistic Society – www.autism.org.uk

Provides information, support and training through a wide range of services for autistic children, young people and adults and their families across the UK. It also provides services for professionals.

Network Autism – www.networkautism.org.uk

A UK-wide online forum and resource base for the sharing of skills, knowledge and practice in the area of autism.

PDA Society – www.pdasociety.org.uk

Provides information, support and training for parents, carers, teachers and individuals with PDA.

Scottish Autism – www.scottishautism.org

The largest provider of autism-specific services in Scotland. It's Right Click programmes provide e-training on a range of subjects including eating.

Young Minds – www.youngminds.org.uk

The UK's leading charity championing the wellbeing and mental health of young people. It provides a range of resources, support and training for young people, their families and professionals.

Index

Page references to Figures or Photographs will be in *italics*

adrenalin 36
amygdala, brain 36
anaemia, iron-deficient 89–90
anorexia nervosa 196, *197*, 198
anxiety
  disgust 77
  'fussy' eaters 44
  hypersensitivity 43, 60, 79
  hypervigilance 44, 53, 54, 61
  impact of 118
  management of 167–70
    breathing exercises
      187–99, 192
    calm and relaxing scripts 189
    challenging anxious
      thinking 185
    in older children 179
    progressive muscle
      relaxation 188–9
    tackling anxious thoughts 185
    tackling body changes 186–9
  at mealtimes 44, 98, 100–1, 143
  negative anxiety cycle 142, 143
  and neophobia 49, 61–2
  of parents/families 113–14, 115
  sensitivity, sensory 49,
    51, 61–2, 64
appearance of food 38–9,
  48, 72, 75, 107
appetite 79–94
  amount of food required
    80–2, 92
  balancing the diet 85–6

decrease in 101
factors stopping a child
    from eating 88–92
  constipation 89–90
  illness 89
  iron-deficient anaemia 90–1
  stress 91–2
  supplementary feeding
    88–9, 93
  tips for parents and
    carers 93–4
hunger 82, 83, 93
  learning to be hungry 84–5
  leaving child to 'go
    hungry' 150–1
  provocation programme 132
  management of 156–8, 177–8
  mindfulness for 178
  regulation and
    compensation 82–3
  responding to cues to eat 83–4
  social influences 87
  stimulating 132
ARFID (Avoidant and
    Restricted Food Intake
    Disorder) 16, 95–112
  acquired 105
  in adults 205
  and anorexia 196, *197*, 198
  with Asperger's syndrome 128
  and children who are
    'just fussy' 105–7
  criteria 98, 108

ARFID (Avoidant and Restricted
    Food Intake Disorder) *cont.*
  defining characteristics 97
  description of child with 98–102
  desensitisation 207
  determining whether
      children have 107–8
  diagnosis 103, 104, 108, 150, 206
  differential diagnoses 102–8
  disgust 99–100
  eating difficulties apart
      from condition 195
  food choices 129, *130*
  'grazing' by affected
      children 157
  hypersensitivity, sensory 137
  medically compromised
      children 104–5
  messy play, benefits of 107
  motivation 133–4, 137
  oral-motor skills, delayed
      in ARFID children
      128, 131, 137
  sensitivity, sensory
      100, 137, 197
  taste trials 190
  tips for parents and
      carers 109–10
  vegetarian and vegan diets 199
  see also autism/autistic
      spectrum; eating
      difficulties (in general);
      hypersensitivity, sensory
aspiration 132
autism/autistic spectrum
  in adolescence 133, 176
  and anorexia 197
  Asperger's syndrome 60
  disgust 148
  eating difficulties apart
      from condition 195
  high-functioning autism 60

hypersensitivity/sensitivity
      59, 60, 62
  and imitation 42, 49
  managing, with younger
      children 155
  mental health issues 203
  rewards and punishments 148
  routines 171
  sameness, desire for 47–8
  sensory overload 159
  tactile hypersensitivity 128
  taste trials 190
  see also ARFID (Avoidant
      and Restricted Food
      Intake Disorder); eating
      difficulties (in general)
Avoidant and Restricted Food
    Intake Disorder *see* ARFID
    (Avoidant and Restricted
    Food Intake Disorder)

bananas 23
beetroot 20
'binge eating' 83
biscuits, preference for 40–1
bite-and-melt/bite-and-dissolve
    foods 28, 31, 57, 128
bitter foods 2, 18, 19–22, 24, 66
blame
  blaming the parents 117
  feelings of 115–16
  impact of 118
  reasons for parents blaming
      themselves 116–17
Blisset, Jackie 45
body scan 178
Boyle, Stephanie 135
brand-loyalty 46, 49, 98,
      99, 104, 164, 200
bread 40, 41, 51, 83, 99, 102
  fortified 102
  sliced/unsliced 165
breast milk 19

breathing exercises 187–8, 192
bribery 45, 49, 147–9, 151
broccoli 19, 23, 66, 127, 146
brown/beige carbohydrate diet 57
Brussels sprouts 19, 20

calorie loads 85, 88, 114, 132
carrots 20
centile lines/charts 80, *81*, 88, 92
cheese 73
chewing skills, developing
    25, 26, 27, 32
Child and Adolescent
    Mental Health Services
    (CAMHS) 168, 198, 203
chocolate 39, 57, 91, 99, 120,
    128, 129, 134, 147
    buttons 43, 129, 164
    milk or dark 24
choking 62, 97, 132, 205
coercion/forcing 45, 49, 140, 141
cognitive behavioural therapy
    (CBT) 185, 191
compensatory eating 83, 89, 93
constipation 89–90
contamination 68–70, *71*, 145, 146
coriander 20
cough reflex 25, 26, 27, 31

dark chocolate 24
depression 202–3
desensitisation 131, 159–64,
    173, 180–3, 192
    ARFID (Avoidant and Restricted
        Food Intake Disorder) 207
    face and lips 161
    hands 160–1
    mouth 161–2
    older children 180–3, 192, 193
    staged 183
    visual 181, 182
    younger children 159–64, 173

developmental age, working
    out 135, 136
*Diagnostic and Statistical
    Manual of Mental Disorders*
    (DSM-5) 97, 103
difference, fear of *see*
    neophobia (onset of fear
    of new/different foods)
disgust 64–78
    anxiety 77
    ARFID (Avoidant and
        Restricted Food Intake
        Disorder) 99–100
    autism/autistic spectrum 148
    awareness of response 185–6
    contamination 68–70, *71*, 145
    cultural factors 68, 77
    distaste 66–8
    evolutionary factors 65
    and exclusion of foods 64
    faeces 67
    foods inciting 148
    hidden foods 12, 46, 71–2, 143–6
    hierarchy of 77
    hypersensitivity,
        sensory 71, 145
    learned 67, 77
    moving on 76
    at others eating 75–6
    refusal to eat 65–6
    response as result of not
        eating a food 74
    rotting flesh 67
    safe foods 72–3
    smell of other people's food 58
    textures 22
    tips for parents and carers 77–8
    unknown foods 96
distaste 66–8
distraction, using 170
dysphagia (difficulties with
    swallowing) 128, 132

early years *see* infancy
and childhood
eating difficulties (in
general) 195–210
eating disorders 69, 196–9
in adults 83
mental health issues 201–3
pathological demand
avoidance 199–201
pica 67, 203–5
tips for parents and
carers 209–10
transition to adulthood 205–8
Einstein, Albert 153
enriched foods 102
environment management 113–25
allowing preferred foods
in schools 123
blame 115–19
eating in school 119–20
health professionals *115*
'healthy eating' policies 120–1
'junk food' and avoidant
eating 121
new 'rule book' for
schools 121–3
parental and family
anxiety 113–14, 115
tips for parents and carers 125
tips for schools 123–4
willingness to try a
new food 132–6
evidence-based practice 15, 153
evolutionary factors, food
preferences 18, 51
appetite regulation 82
disgust 65, 67
onset of fear of new/different
foods 35, 37, 49
exclusion diets, avoiding
where necessary 40
exclusive milk diets 131, 137

facial expression/tone
of voice 23, 32

fat in food, preference for 24
fear response 35–7
'fight or flight response'
36, 54, 91, 184, 189
finger foods 55
fish 21, 23
food aversions *see* refusal to
eat particular foods
food cues, responding to 83–4
food preferences
allowing preferred foods
in schools 123
biscuits 40–1
developing 17
evolutionary factors 18,
35, 37, 49, 51
fat 24
flavours of favourite foods 39
persistence of 21
tastes 19–21
usual, of 'fussy' children 20
withholding preferred
foods 101, 146–7, 151
food requirements 80–2, 92
foods children averse to,
vegetables 40–1
fortified foods 102, 114
fromage frais 24
'fussy' children
and ARFID 105–7
personal experiences
of author 9
reasons for behaviour 18
restricted eating patterns
15–16, 46–7
usual foods preferences 20

'gag' response 25, 26, 55,
62, 96, 107, 123
green vegetables 19–22
growth, health and nutrition
management
with older children 176–7
with younger children 155–6

growth charts 80
guilt 118, 140

harder foods 25
Harris, Gillian 9–11, 16
health management *see*
    growth, health and
    nutrition management
health professionals 96,
    97, 114, *115*
'healthy eating' policies 120–1
hiding new foods 12, 46,
    71–2, 143–6, 151
home-prepared foods 22–3
hunger 59, 82, 83, 93
    learning to be hungry 84–5
    leaving child to 'go
        hungry' 150–1
    provocation programme 132
hypersensitivity, sensory
    and anxiety/neophobia
        43, 60, 79
    ARFID (Avoidant and
        Restricted Food Intake
        Disorder) 95–6, 137
    and autism 60, 62
    defining 53
    difficult and easy textures 57
    disgust 71, 145
    feeding and eating behaviours,
        affecting 54–6
    vs. hyposensitivity 59
    personal experiences
        of author 9
    sight 43
    tactile 127–8, 131
    tastes, acceptance of 79
    textures 137
    visual 144
    see also ARFID (Avoidant
        and Restricted Food
        Intake Disorder); autism/
        autistic spectrum;
        sensitivity, sensory

hypervigilance 44, 53,
    54, 61, 100, 145
hyposensitivity, sensory 59–60, 62

illness 89
imitating others 41–2, 49, 149–50
    failure to imitate others, in
        restricted eating patterns
        42, 87, 100, 149, 152
infancy and childhood
    coping with textures 24–5
    eating skills, developing 17, 25
    food preferences 17
    mixed foods 26–7, 37
    problems with textures 31
    progression of textured
        foods *29–31*
    responsive feeding 23–4
    senses 22–3
    tastes 19–21
    tips for parents and carers 32–3
    usual food preferences of
        'fussy' children 20
    see also appetite; ARFID
        (Avoidant and Restricted
        Food Intake Disorder);
        disgust; neophobia (onset
        of fear of new/different
        foods); senses/sensory
        factors; sensitivity, sensory
interoception 53, 59, 62, 150
iron-deficient anaemia 89–90

leafy vegetables 21, 22
learned safety 18, 47, 51, 60, 66
lumps in foods, introducing
    25, 27, 55, 129

Mason, Sarah 11
mealtimes, as source of anxiety
    44, 98, 100–1, 143
meat-substitutes 74
medically compromised
    children 104–5

mental health issues 201–3
messy play, benefits of
107, 156, 163
metabolic rate 82
milk chocolate 24
milk diets, exclusive 131
mindfulness 177, 178
mixed foods 26–7, 37, 71
motivation (children with
ARFID) 133–4, 137
moving on
common categories of
accepted foods and
sensory sensitivity *130*
developmental age,
working out 135, 136
disgust 76
expectations, managing 136–7
food choices, in ARFID
children 129, *130*, 131
getting older 134–6
motivation 133–4, 137
neophobia 41–3
readiness 126–38
tips for parents and carers 138
tolerating textures 126–32
see also ARFID (Avoidant
and Restricted Food
Intake Disorder)
mushrooms 10, 46, 72, 127

negative anxiety cycle 142, 143
neophobia (fear of new
foods) 34–50, 62
age of child 47, 48
anxiety 49
ARFID (Avoidant and
Restricted Food Intake
Disorder) 99, 149
children with restricted
eating patterns 46–7
extreme response 37, 43
failure in early learning 48
fear response 35–7

and game playing 43, 50
'general' 101
genetic factors 37
growing out of 49
mixed foods 37
moving on from neophobic
response 41–3
prevalence in some children
as opposed to others 43–4
sameness, desire for 47–8
second year 34
sensitivity, sensory 49,
51, 61–2, 64, 101
strength of response 37
tactics tried by parents 45–6
tips for parents and
carers 49–50
understanding neophobic
response 37–40
see also ARFID (Avoidant
and Restricted Food
Intake Disorder); autism/
autistic spectrum;
hypersensitivity, sensory
new foods, acceptance/
willingness to try 21, 36
noise, sensitivity to 58
nutrition management *see*
growth, health and
nutrition management

obsessive compulsive disorder
(OCD) 68, 201–2, 209
older children
acceptance of new foods 21
anxiety management 184–93
appetite management 177–8
autism and teenage years 176
becoming independent 192–3
behaviour management 189
desensitisation 180–3, 192, 193
interventions with 175–94
managing growth, health
and nutrition 176–7

overload 180
rigidity management 179
sensory issues 180–3
staged desensitisation 183
taste trials 190–2, 193
tips for parents and carers 194
transition to adulthood 205–8
oleander 19
oral-motor skills, delayed in
    ARFID children 128, 131, 137
overeating 59, 83, 158
    social cues 87

packaging, changes in 39, 144, *145*
parents and carers
    anxieties of 113–14, 115
    blaming 117
    facial expression/tone
        of voice 23, 32
    reasons not to blame 118–19
    reasons for parents blaming
        themselves 116–17, 139
    tactics tried by *see* strategies
        used by parents/carers
    tips for 32–3, 49–50, 93–4,
        109–10, 125, 138, 174
pathological demand avoidance
    (PDA) 199–201, 209
    PDA-friendly strategies 200
pica 67, 203–5
practice-based evidence 153
preferences, food *see*
    food preferences
prefrontal cortex, brain 36
pressure to eat 140–3
    encouragement 140
    guilt 140
    persuasion/prompting 140, 141
progressive muscle
    relaxation 188–9
prototypes 38
pureed food 28, 98–9, 128, 131
putrid foods 22

reflux 31, 53
refusal to eat particular foods 10
    appearance of food 38–9, 48
    in ARFID (Avoidant and
        Restricted Food Intake
        Disorder) 107
    disgust 65–6
    familiarity 40–1
    reasons for 38, 77
relaxation activities 169, 186
responsive feeding 23–4
restricted eating patterns 32, 46–7
    anxiety at mealtimes 44,
        98, 100–1, 143
    ARFID (Avoidant and Restricted
        Food Intake Disorder)
        95, 98, 109, 171, 195
    avoidant children with 96–7
    balancing the diet 86
    binge eating 83
    chocolate intake 91
    clinic visits 126
    exclusion diets 40
    failure to imitate others
        42, 87, 100, 149, 152
    inappropriate substances 67
    intakes 40, 83, 87
    mental health issues 209
    neophobia (fear of new
        foods) 46–7, 51
    school pressures 92
    self-awareness issues 53
    sensory issues 59, 60, 64
    stressful periods 91–2, 93, 155
    see also ARFID (Avoidant
        and Restricted Food
        Intake Disorder)
rewards 45–6, 147–9, 151, 191
rigidity management 164–7, 179
routines and rituals,
    managing 170–3, 179

safe foods 18, 21, 72–3, 95, 96
    foods 'known to be safe' 99
    learned safety 18, 47, 51, 60, 66

salty foods 21
sameness, desire for 47–8
schools
  allowing preferred foods in 123
  dining halls, avoiding 76
  eating in 119–20
  tips for 123
second year 34, 109
second-stage baby foods 26
senses/sensory factors
  31, 51–63, 62
  functions of the senses 52
  interoception 53, 59, 62, 150
  overload 159, 180
  sight see sight
  smell see smell
  sound 58
  touch 42, 43, 53, 54, 107
  see also sensitivity,
    sensory; textures
sensitivity, sensory 32
  and acceptance of food 64
  anxiety and neophobia 49,
    51, 61–2, 64, 101
  ARFID (Avoidant and
    Restricted Food Intake
    Disorder) 100, 137, 197
  and autism 60
  contamination 68
  defining 52–4
  details, over-emphasis
    on 43, 62, 64
  in early infancy 27
  and hidden foods 46
  hypersensitivity see
    hypersensitivity, sensory
  hyposensitivity 59–60
  managing sensory
    issues 158–64
  messy play, benefits of 56
  noise 58
  older children, interventions
    with 180–3

reluctance to try textured
  foods 34
wider picture, failing
  to see 43, 62, 64
see also hypersensitivity,
  sensory
Shea, Elizabeth 11–13, 16
side-to-side tongue movement,
  chewing 25, 26, 27, 55
sight 22–3, 43, 58–9
  appearance of food 38–9, 48
  visual hypersensitivity 144
sight of food see
  appearance of food
slimy foods/textures 10
  acceptance or rejection in
    infancy childhood 18, 21–2,
    24, 57, 69, 73, 74, 76, 77, 79
  avoidant and restrictive
    eating 107, 127
  disgust 70
smell 22–3, 43, 99
  disgust 69, 72
  sensory factors and food
    acceptance 53, 54,
    57–9, 58, 61, 62
social eating, 'rules' 208
solid food, complementary 19, 32
sound 58, 75
sour foods 19, 21, 24
spreading the sets 165–7
staged desensitisation 183
sticky fingers game 164
'strangers', fear of 35
strategies used by parents/carers
  bribing 45, 49, 147–9, 151
  forcing 45, 49, 140, 141
  hiding new foods 12, 46,
    71–2, 143–6, 151
  imitating others 149–50
  ineffective 139–52
  knowing what not to do 151
  leaving child to 'go
    hungry' 150–1

negative anxiety cycle 142, 143
persuasion/prompting 140, 141
pressure to eat 140–3
prompting 45, 140
rewards 45–6, 147–9, 191
sitting in front of a
new food 140
threats 140
tips for parents and carers 152
withholding preferred
foods 146–7
stress 54, 91–2
stringy textures 18, 22, 24
supplementary feeding
88–9, 93, 131
swallowing 25, 61–2
dysphagia (difficulties with
swallowing) 128, 132
sweet foods 19

tastes 19–21, 22, 39, 62, 79
taste trials 142, 190–2, 193
see also bitter foods; sour
foods; sweet foods; umami
textures
acceptance 25
biscuits, preference for 41
changes in 39
contamination 69, 71
coping with 24–5
delay in introducing lumpy
or solid-textured foods
27, 34, 54, 103
difficult 57, 127
disgust 69
dry 56
easier 28, 57
hypersensitivity 137
mixed 57
moving on with 129
new, introducing 24
problems with 31
progression of textured
foods 29–31

sensitivity to, in ARFID 127–9
slimy see slimy foods/textures
sticky wet 56
stringy 18, 22, 24
tolerating 126–32
vegetables, aversion to 41
see also hypersensitivity,
sensory; lumps in foods,
introducing; pureed food;
sensitivity, sensory
touch 42, 43, 53, 54, 107
tactile hypersensitivity
127–8, 131
toxicity, and bitter tastes 19
tube-feeding 98, 101, 104, 105, 131

umami 19

vegetables
aversion to 40–1
bitter taste 2, 19, 24
bribing to eat 45
constipation from
insufficient intake 89
desired by parents to be
consumed 19–20, 65
hidden 12, 71
leafy 21, 22
neophobic responses 43
raw 203
refusal by child 22, 46
smell 99
sweet 20
see also specific vegetables,
such as broccoli
vegetarian and vegan diets 21, 199
visualisation 189
vomiting 11, 62, 77, 89, 96, 97, 123
fear of 90

weak central coherence 149
withholding preferred
foods 101, 146–7
wrappers 39

yoghurt 24, 28, 102
younger children, interventions
    with 153–74
  anxiety management 167–70
  appetite management 156–8
  autism management 155
  daily eating schedules 157
  desensitisation 159–64, 173
  distraction, using 170
  evidence-based practice 153
  growth, health and
      nutrition 155–6
  messy play 163

prior to starting 154
relaxation activities 169
rigidity management 164–7
routines and rituals,
    managing 170–3
'same as' analogy, using 166–7
sensory issues 158–64
spreading the sets 165–7
sticky fingers game 164
tips for parents and carers 174
see also older children,
    interventions with